THE BLOODY BATTLE FOR

SURIBACHI

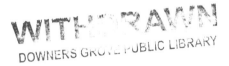

Downers Grove Public Library
1050 Curtiss St.
Downers Grove, IL 60515

THE BLOODY BATTLE FOR
SURIBACHI

The Amazing Story of Iwo Jima That Inspired *Flags of Our Fathers*

By Richard Wheeler

With a Foreword by Robert Lorenz

Skyhorse Publishing

www.skyhorsepublishing.com

Library of Congress Cataloging-in-Publication Data

Wheeler, Richard.
The bloody battle for Suribachi: the amazing story of Iwo Jima that inspired flags of our fathers/by Richard Wheeler; with a foreword by Robert Lorenz.
    p. cm.
  Includes bibliographical references and index.
  Originally published: New York : Crowell, 1965.
  ISBN-13: 978-1-60239-180-2 (pbk. : alk. paper)
  ISBN-10: 1-60239-180-7 (pbk. : alk. paper)
 1. Wheeler, Richard. 2. Iwo Jima, Battle of, Japan, 1945—Personal narratives, American. 3. United States. Marine Corps—Biography. 4. Marines—United States—Biography. I. Title.

D767.99.I9 W44 2007
940.54'26—dc22

10 9 8 7 6 5 4 3 2 1

Printed in Canada

This special edition of
The Bloody Battle for Suribachi
is dedicated, with the deepest appreciation,
to my cousin, Judge Jacqueline L. Russell.

Her steadfast encouragement, resourceful
thinking, and hands-on assistance were
essentially linked to the volume's production.

CONTENTS

MAPS

FOREWORD

Dear Reader,

Of all the books, documentaries and recorded interviews we consulted while preparing to film *Flags of Our Fathers* and *Letters from Iwo Jima*, *The Bloody Battle for Suribachi* stood out as an exceptional resource. Richard Wheeler's detailed, thoughtful and dramatic firsthand account of the struggle to capture Mount Suribachi is both horrifying and thrilling. So thorough and vivid is the story that Clint Eastwood asked all the principal actors in *Flags* to read it.

History is fortunate that a writer as eloquent as Richard Wheeler was present during the battle of Iwo Jima and lived to tell about it. He serves admirably as a voice for all the men who endured that savage fight and countless others throughout World War II.

Sincerely,

Robert Lorenz
Producer, *Flags of Our Fathers* and *Letters from Iwo Jima*

PREFACE

As an aspiring author, I enlisted in the U.S. Marines at the start of WWII seeking a story worth writing about, and I chanced to become involved in one of the greatest stories of the time. I was a rifleman, a corporal, in the 250-man company that raised both flags on the summit of Mount Suribachi, Iwo Jima—the small flag that officially proclaimed the volcano's capture, and the large replacement flag that became the subject of Joe Rosenthal's incomparable photo, taken for the Associated Press.

The Bloody Battle for Suribachi, largely a personal narrative, was first published in 1965. There is no other book like it. I was in the front lines with the flag-raising guys, and I gathered my impressions of the fighting (as one reviewer phrased it) "while a split-second from death."

Severely wounded, I began writing my first account of the Suribachi assault while lying in a hospital bed swathed in bandages tinged with blood, my memories disturbingly vivid.

Much of my supplementary material was secured by means of talks and letter-exchanges with surviving comrades during the months immediately following the battle.

Since the close of WWII, Iwo Jima's notability has not only been maintained; it has grown. At the present time, thanks largely to James Bradley's best-selling book, coupled with the movies that have followed—*Flags of Our* Fathers and *Letters from Iwo Jima*—the battle is rising from one of great fame to one of legend. It is winning a place among the best-known conflicts in the history of warfare.

For my part, I've decided that the time is exactly right for the publication of a "special edition" of *The Bloody Battle for Suribachi*. There is a lot in this book that was not in the original edition: a more powerful selection of photographs, a sheaf of rhymes, an appendix made up of items never before published that I extracted from my collection of Iwo Jima keepsakes, and an account of the 3rd Platoon's "sunset muster" in Washington, D.C., in 2006.

Perhaps I'd better explain the rhymes. During my long career as a writer, I once earned a part of my income as a poet, placing hundreds of pieces, mostly light in nature, among the nation's periodicals. My Iwo rhymes reflect no lightness.

At age 85, I feel very lucky to have survived to enjoy all of this new attention centered upon the battle. And it's gratifying that I've retained the mental strength I need to be a productive part of events.

My days on earth, I'm well aware, grow very short. But what a glorious time for an old Iwo Jima Marine to be making his exit!

Richard Wheeler
July 2007

THE BLOODY BATTLE FOR

SURIBACHI

FORTY-SIX MARINES

Iwo Jima was a gray silhouette in the dawn of February 19, 1945, when we got our first look at it. Our attack force had arrived off the island during the night and had merged with the mighty support force that had been bombarding Japanese defenses for the past three days.

The big guns of the battleships and cruisers flashed sharply as they boomed their pre-H-hour shells toward the positions overlooking the landing zone. Also in action were rocket-armed LCIs whose missiles left white backblasts as they whooshed from their launchers. The target areas teemed with red bursts and rumbled steadily, and dark columns of smoke and dust drifted skyward.

From the deck of our transport we forty-six men of the 3rd Platoon of Company E, 2nd Battalion, 28th Marines, scanned the island apprehensively. We expected it to prove tough, for it was part of Japan's inner defense line. It lay only 660 nautical miles from Tokyo. We knew that its seven and a half square miles held more than twenty thousand crack troops and a maze of ingenious fortifications. Its highest point was Mount Suribachi, an extinct volcano that made up its southwestern tip. This heavily fortified elevation would be our regiment's first objective.

Fate had picked the 3rd Platoon for an important role in Mount Suribachi's capture. Those of our men who managed to escape death or injury would plant the first American flag on the volcano's summit. This would be one of the great moments of World War II.

Unfortunately, two hours after the flag was planted it would be replaced by a larger one, and a striking photograph taken of the second raising would win a popularity that would relegate the original act to obscurity. The second raising, in addition to becoming the subject of a huge statue in the nation's capital, would inspire a great many writings and would be featured in a number of moving picture and television productions. But the 3rd Platoon's story, in spite of its significance and its drama, would remain relatively untold. The survivors of the second raising would become national figures, while those of the first would be forgotten.

But we had no way of knowing any of this on the morning of February 19, 1945. We were then only a typical rifle platoon, one small part of a regimental combat team.

Our regiment was a new one, having been organized as an element of the 5th Marine Division at Camp Pendleton, California, only a year before. We were commanded by Colonel Harry B. "Harry the Horse" Liversedge, a tall ruggedly handsome officer who had fought the Japanese in the Solomon Islands. Lieutenant Colonel Robert H. Williams was second in command. Though we would be going into action as a unit for the first time, our ranks had been formed around a nucleus of combat veterans, including former Marine Raiders and Marine Paratroopers.

Our members had assembled at Camp Pendleton from many points. Some had sailed from Pacific combat areas, while others had checked in from stateside hospitals where they had been recuperating from wounds. Some had come from special training centers and some from naval bases where they had been serving with guard units. And some had reported directly from boot camp.

Basic training was an important part of the backgrounds of all of us. It had done more than indoctrinate us in the military fundamentals and toughen our muscles. It had steeped us in discipline and had given us a keen confidence in the Marine Corps as a fighting force.

My own boot camp hitch was two years behind me, but its rigors, abasements, frustrations and fleeting moments of pride were well remembered. I had come straight from a civilian life of comfort, security and individuality, a life in which I was endowed with "certain inalienable rights." And suddenly I was just another boot, a drill instructor's puppet, an object of derision and harassment, an American with no rights at all. I was plunged into a frantic-paced schedule of unfamiliar and highly demanding activities. My health was jeopardized. I was deliberately angered and humiliated. My adequacy was constantly questioned. Could I prove that I was a man and not merely a sniveling boy? Had I the stamina and the gumption to make it through the program without cracking?

There were sixty-one of us in boot camp Platoon 154—sixty-one clip-haired, bungling, sadly confused nonentities. We were subjected to long hours of calisthenics, hiking and double timing; close order, extended order and guard duty drill; and bayonet, hand grenade and gas mask practice. And we had to listen to a barrage of lectures on topics that ranged from weapons care to venereal disease.

We also spent two weeks on the rifle range. This involved our hiking many miles a day and our doing a lot of contortionistic "snapping in" that left us with acutely complaining muscles. The hike back to camp in the afternoon, when we were already worn, was always grueling. And our instructor didn't help the situation when he hurled the old taunt: "Anybody who's tired of walking can start running!"

We experienced many other discomforts and annoyances. We shivered during our pre-dawn roll call and we sweltered during later activities in the sun. Colds and mysterious fevers multiplied among us. Our aching muscles were further abused by vaccine injections. We were often deprived of sufficient sleep, and then were disciplined for nodding during our lecture periods. When we responded too slowly to a command we were sometimes accelerated by a rap from our instructor's swagger stick, and we were occasionally even "handled" when we made him angry.

Boot Camp Platoon 154 (author in 2nd row, 4th from left) "graduated" in February, 1942, soon after the war began. The author had been lured into enlisting by the slogan, "U.S. Marines—First to Fight" (see panel at bottom of photo). In his youthful lightheartedness, the author had left his hometown with the announcement, "I'm going away to war and get killed a little."

But after boot camp he found himself assigned to two years of guard duty on West Coast military bases. His most dangerous assignment was the directing of traffic at busy intersections. His letters home exuded shame.

The war was nearly over when things began to look up. The author was assigned to a combat division, became part of a frenzy of training, then sailed away to Iwo Jima. There he experienced three days of the fiercest kind of fighting, was scared out of his wits, and ended up a very bloody stretcher case.

Later in 1945, while he was lying in a stateside hospital bed, suffering but finally PROUD, he told himself: "I was saved for the worst battle in Marine Corps history. Now I can go home with HONOR."

The author's pleasure was boundless when a neighbor lady, recalling his parting words, greeted him with: "How did it feel to get killed a little?"

Marine Corps Photo

Penalties for failure and neglect were sternly administered. They involved such ordeals as our double timing until we were nearly exhausted and our holding our rifles at arm's length until the tension and pain became unbearable. If a man let his whiskers become noticeable he was ordered to shave "dry." There was a particularly humiliating punishment for witless blunders. The offender was made to stand before the platoon with a bucket inverted over his head and was obliged to shout, until the instructor was appeased, "I am a shit-head! I am a shit-head!"

Our day usually didn't end until 10:00 P.M., and this allowed us only six and a half hours of sleep. The group I was tented with got a little less. One of our number was a young minister from Tennessee, and each night after taps he would kneel by his cot and deliver a long, impassioned prayer. But the rest of us didn't find Private William T. Carter's religious fervor objectionable. We couldn't help but be warmed by his practice of making a special appeal for each of us. He not only prayed for our general welfare but asked that we be guided safely through the war.

Rigorous as the training was, it had its bright spots. Much of it was interesting, and we experienced a thrill of satisfaction each time we managed to master one of the more difficult challenges it presented. The lecture periods provided us the breaks we needed from physical activity. We nearly always enjoyed our meals; our appetites were sharp and the food was good. There were evenings when we were granted two free hours to attend an outdoor moving picture.

And we could look forward to mail call once a day—though any man who received more than one or two letters was censured by the instructor for keeping his home ties too strong.

Each Sunday we attended church. But most of the sermons seemed strangely out of keeping with the Lord's teachings. We heard little about the universal brotherhood of man under a universally loving father. The worship was keyed to the needs of war. Our minister addressed his petitions not so much to the Jesus of gentleness and compassion as to the Jesus who could be roused to "righteous indignation." The Lord was entreated to help us defeat our enemies. The Cross must precede us into battle. Though it would be the same cross that symbolized salvation through faith and the milder virtues, it must double as a mace. But this sort of supplication to the Prince of Peace was hardly something new under the Sunday sun.

When our training program ended, there were still fifty-eight of the original sixty-one men in the platoon. We had lost one through a leg injury and two through sickness. This was a good showing but was really no better than it should have been. We had entered boot camp only after we'd had three physical examinations, two of which were comprehensive. And we had also undergone a psychiatric examination. We had been found physically and mentally strong enough for the training. Moreover, most of us were youths who had

KITANO POINT

KANGOKU ROCK

OKITA

382-B

ONISHI

AIRFIELD NO. 3 (UNDER CONSTRUCTION)

ORANGE I O-2

ORANGE 2

382-A

MOTOYAMA O

382-C

KAMA ROCK

WHITE I

AIRFIELD NO. 2

382

WHITE 2 O-1

TACHIIWA POINT O-2

BROWN I

MINAMI

BROWN 2

QUARRY

PURPLE

AIRFIELD NO. I

O-1

EAST BOAT BASIN

BLUE 2

23 ≡ 25

BLUE I (1/25 and 3/25 landed abreast)

YELLOW 2

YELLOW I

28 ≡ 27

RED 2
FUTATSU ROCK
RED I

MOUNT SURIBACHI

GREEN

LANDING PLAN

TOBIISHI POINT

1000   500   0   1000
YARDS

Position of 28th Marines on left flank, near Mount Suribachi's base. Landing plan calls for the 1st and 2nd Battalions to land in column, each occupying a two-company front. The regiment's 3rd Battalion is not shown here because the plan called for it to be held in floating reserve.

Alternate landing areas are indicated on west coast. Alternate plan was drawn up because it was feared that D-day surf conditions might make the preferred landing on the east coast unfeasible.

The line curving to the right from the landing beaches is the dividing line between zones of action of the 4th and 5th Marine Divisions.

The lines that cross the island (O-1 and O-2) are initial and secondary objective lines. Attacking units are to be halted here for control, coordination, and further orders.

enlisted in the Marines partly for the purpose of establishing our manhood, so we were able to maintain a do-or-die incentive.

Our making it through the program stirred us to considerable pride and elation. We had stood up under the stiff discipline, we had proved we could take it physically, and we had absorbed the military fundamentals satisfactorily. We

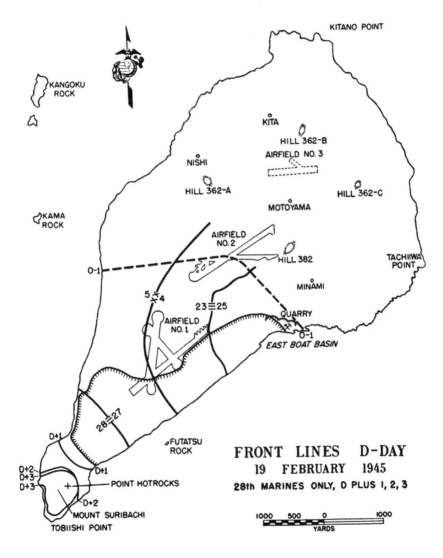

FRONT LINES D-DAY
19 FEBRUARY 1945
28th MARINES ONLY, D PLUS 1, 2, 3

D-day front lines for the whole landing force are shown by the line with the right-angle strokes attached to it. Then the progress of all other units is ignored in favor of the 28th Marines and the assault on Mount Suribachi. Indicated are the regiment's front lines on D-day, D-plus-1, 2, and 3. (The flag was raised on the morning of D-plus-4.) The two "D-plus-3s" at the left of the volcano show that it has been surrounded, as though by a noose.

had qualified ourselves for admission into a highly capable and fine-traditioned fighting outfit. We were now full-fledged United States Marines.

Though we expected to be assigned at once to an infantry division, our platoon was one of those selected for distribution among guard detachments. I myself served two years at naval bases on the West Coast and in Alaska before finally being ordered to Camp Pendleton.

We men of the 5th Marine Division spent the first half of our year of combat training in California and the last half in the Hawaiian Islands. Our schedule included a wide variety of both land and sea exercises. When our higher-echelon officers learned, four months before D-day, that Iwo Jima would be our objective they kept the information to themselves but ordered that we be taught more about attacking fortified positions and reducing bunkers and pillboxes. They also arranged for added emphasis to be placed on the use of supporting arms. Because the job of assaulting Mount Suribachi was assigned to the 28th Marines, we of this regiment suddenly found ourselves with a mountain to climb during each of our field problems. Without knowing it, we often executed the actual scheme of maneuver we would use on Iwo.

Of the forty-six of us in the 3rd Platoon of Company E, 2nd Battalion, about a dozen were ex-raiders and ex-paratroopers, while the rest of us had seen no action. We were organized into three rifle squads and one assault squad, the latter being armed with flame throwers, demolitions and a bazooka. Our leaders were 1st Lieutenant John K. Wells, Platoon Sergeant Ernest I. Thomas and Sergeant Henry O. Hansen. The last, our right guide, was the only one with front-line combat experience.

Lieutenant Wells was a tall dark-haired Texan. He was twenty-three but looked older, having strong features that had been matured early by the southwestern sun and wind. His habit of mixing freely with the enlisted men made him a popular leader, and we referred to him, among ourselves, as "J.K." or the inevitable "Tex." Though he liked to tilt his overseas cap forward carelessly and walk around with a don't-give-a-damn look, he was serious-natured. He enjoyed discussing the art of warfare, and his approach to the topic was often dramatic. He once told us, with a resolute expression and a raised fist: "Give me fifty men who aren't afraid to die, and I can take *any* position!"

Those of us who intended to be careful with our lives didn't know what to make of this heroic pronouncement. Sergeant Kenneth D. "Katie" Midkiff, an easygoing West Virginian who had seen action with the paratroopers, admitted to his squad that the lieutenant's attitude had him a little worried.

"He wants fifty men who aren't afraid to die," Midkiff said ruefully. Then he pointed at a man he had picked at random and added, "And do you know what? *You're* one of the fifty!"

Wells once obtained a paper-bound book that dealt with the sweep of the Mongols across Asia in the thirteenth century, and he carried it in his pocket and dipped into it during free moments. His comments about its strategic and tactical content prompted us, for a time, to give him a new designation among ourselves. We converted his initials "J.K." into "Jenghiz Khan."

We found our lieutenant colorful and likeable—and puzzling. He talked like a dedicated fighting man and his leadership on the training field was

Lieutenant John Keith Wells.

Studio Photo

competent, but we couldn't help but wonder what he'd be like when the shooting started.

Platoon Sergeant Thomas came from Tallahassee, Florida. His home stood very near the governor's mansion, he told us. Only twenty, he was five-feet-ten, broad-shouldered and boyishly good-looking. His most prominent feature was his kinky, close-cropped, almost-platinum-blond hair. Though he was ordinarily soft-spoken he had no trouble raising his voice when the need arose. He had been a Marine for only a short time but his quick mind and his aptitude for leadership had enabled him to advance rapidly. His several months of service as a boot camp drill instructor had earned him the nickname "Boots," but we also referred to him, with liking and admiration, as "Thomas the Tiger."

Sergeant Hansen, who was about twenty-five, came from Somerville, Massachusetts. He was of medium-height, slender and clean-cut, and he had a way of looking natty even in fatigue clothes. His tentmates dubbed him "The Count," but the rest of us called him "Harry" or "Hank." Though he was less forceful than Wells and Thomas he was alert and dependable. He had proved his mettle during his stint with the paratroopers.

Our platoon was made up of men from many states and it spoke with a mixture of accents. Its nationality was various, as suggested by this selection of names: Adrian, Breitenstein, Dyce, Eller, Espenes, Fredotovich, Gaylord, Hagstrom, Hipp, Ignatowski, Jefferson, Kurelik, Lavelle, McNulty, Panizo, Rozek, Scheperle, Schott, Ward. In addition to a full-blooded American Indian we had a man who was born in the Hawaiian Islands and another who was born in Spain.

Numerous backgrounds were represented. There were farmers and ranchers, former members of the Civilian Conservation Corps, a former merchant seaman, a bank clerk, the manager of a five-and-ten-cent store, a truck driver, a newspaper apprentice. Some of our number had joined the Marines immediately after graduating from high school, while others had interrupted college studies. We had a serious art student, Corporal Robert A. Leader, who had been attending the Boston Museum of Fine Arts when he decided to enlist. Tall, fair-complexioned and reddish-haired, Leader wasn't at all "arty." He was clear-minded and practical, as Yankees are supposed to be, and he made a sturdy Marine.

The platoon's oldest man was Corporal Everett M. Lavelle, of Bellingham, Washington. A career Marine, he was only in his late thirties but was graying at the temples, and we considered him mature enough to be called "Pappy" and "Old Man." Pfc. James A. Robeson, also from Washington (Chewelah), was our youngest member. He was eighteen but looked even younger and had been given the nickname "Chick."

Most of our dozen ex-raiders and ex-paratroopers were twenty-five or under but were seasoned campaigners. A typical record was that of Corporal Harold

The Suribachi assault at its successful conclusion. Symbol indicates that battalions of the 28th Marines are occupying the volcano area.

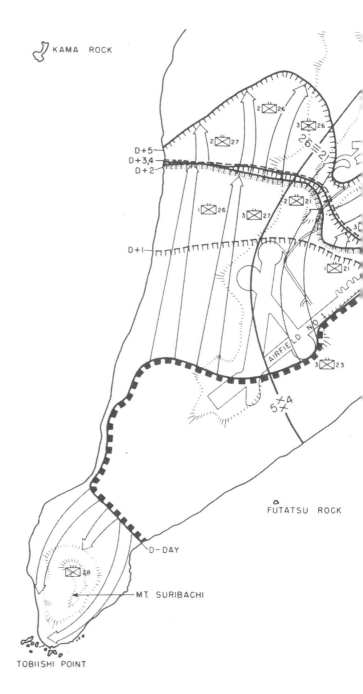

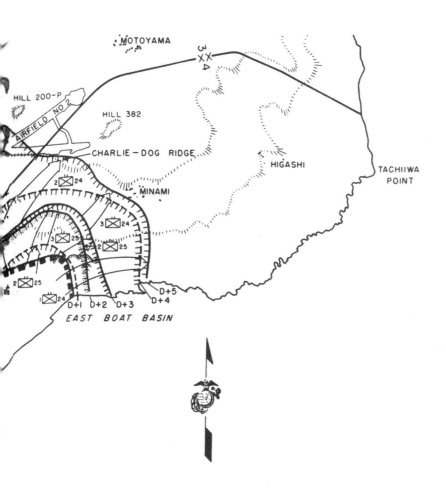

PROGRESS OF THE ATTACK

FRONT LINES D-DAY -- D-PLUS 5

NOTE: ARROWS ON ALL MAPS INDICATE ONLY
GENERAL DIRECTION OF ATTACK, NOT ACTUAL
FRONTAGES OF UNITS

P. Keller, of Brooklyn, Iowa. He had served with the 2nd Raider Battalion in four Pacific engagements, including the daring Makin raid, and had been wounded in the assault on Bougainville. Keller and the other veterans were nearly all able and cool-headed and had the quiet assurance of men who know

Robert Leader and Howard Snyder on liberty in Hawaii. Snyder, a store manager in civilian life and the author's squad leader and best friend, was killed on Iwo. Leader, an art student when he enlisted, was critically wounded but survived to become an art professor at the University of Notre Dame and an internationally known expert on church-related art and design.

Studio Photo

they have proved their courage. Those of us who had seen no action regarded them with considerable respect and got a comfortable feeling out of having them with us.

Though our unit was well disciplined it held one confirmed rebel. Pfc. Donald J. Ruhl, of Joliet, Montana, often grumbled about orders he considered unreasonable and he sometimes made trouble for himself by trying to ignore them. Impatient to get into combat, he chafed at the repetitions in our schedule. He viewed his helmet as a useless trapping and wore it only at the insistence of his squad leader. His attitude earned him the platoon's criticism from time to time, but he seemed to feel that he shouldn't be judged until he'd been tested on the battlefield.

We had two Navy hospital corpsmen with us: Pharmacist's Mate 2nd Class John H. Bradley, of Wisconsin, and Pharmacist's Mate 3rd Class Clifford R. Langley, a Missourian. They lived and trained with the platoon and dressed in Marine uniforms. In appearance they differed from the rest of us only in that they wore Navy-type chevrons.

During our months together we became a close-knit group and formed some fast friendships. We got along well in spite of our constant shoulder-to-shoulder contact and our frequent exposure to field hardships and other vexations. We knew that our battlefield chances depended to a great degree on our capacity for teamwork, so instead of taking the edge off our nerves by snapping at each other we attacked the System. We complained about our rations, the restrictions, the working parties, the repeated inspections. Serious arguments were few and there were no fist fights. Most of the time there existed a gratifying comradeship and solidarity.

We shared a host of experiences. Many were routine and tedious, but some were a source of interest and excitement. In addition to training with rifles, we operated flame-throwers, threw hand grenades, fired rockets and set off demolitions. We went on countless hikes, bivouacs and field problems, and we often worked in coordination with machine gun, mortar, artillery and tank units. The training took on an added hazard when these support units used live ammunition.

Our aptitude with our entrenching tools was once tested in a bizarre manner. We were ordered to dig deep foxholes and sit in them while Sherman tanks rumbled over us. Our leaders reasoned that we might sometime have to undergo a similar onslaught by Japanese tanks. Only one of us failed this test. The walls of the man's foxhole crumbled about him and he was buried up to his neck. But we found him unhurt when we dug him out.

During our invasion rehearsals we usually disembarked from our troop transport by going over its rail and climbing down a rope net into a landing craft that was waiting below. In a heavy sea, with the ship rolling and the landing craft dipping, this wasn't easily done—particularly since we were always bearing full combat gear. Sometimes, as we reached the bottom of the net and tried to step off, the landing craft would suddenly drop many feet—or would leap up, perhaps to bump us painfully. Once aboard, we often bobbed around in the sea for a couple of hours before heading for the beach or returning to the transport. These hours were always unpleasant, even for those who didn't mind the motion. The landing vessels were not only confining but they droned loudly and gave off disagreeable oil fumes.

We fought a score of wind-fanned grass fires in California and we bivouacked on a Hawaiian Island desert that was the abode of an astonishing number of black widow spiders. The latter area had some exceptionally dry spots. We once hiked a roadway that was literally calf-deep with dust. The desert's bright feature was a type of cactus that bore a delicious red pear. But the fruit was covered with patches of tiny spines, and however carefully we pared away its skin we nearly always wound up with a prickly tongue and palate.

Our most unusual experience occurred while our regiment was engaging in several days of mock warfare with another 5th Division regiment. The maneuver involved the liberal use of blank rifle ammunition, and we opposing combat teams did a lot of shooting at each other. One afternoon while our platoon was busy firing at a unit on a ridge about two hundred yards away, we were surprised to see one of its men rise and hasten toward us. He turned out to be a platoon leader, and he was in a rage.

"Who the hell is using live ammunition over here?" he demanded. "One of my men has just been killed!"

This amounted to an accusation of manslaughter, and our battalion commander was summoned. He ordered us back to camp and we were restricted to our tent area while an armorer fired our rifles into a mattress and compared the recovered bullets with the one taken from the dead man's body. We were all exonerated when no match resulted. Further investigations revealed nothing, but during the battle for Iwo Jima the mystery was cleared up in an unexpected way. A fatally wounded man from the victim's own platoon confessed to having fired the shot—intentionally, out of hatred.

We boarded the *Missoula,* an attack transport, at Hilo, Hawaii, about six weeks before D-day. After taking part in extensive landing exercises among the Hawaiian Islands from January 12 to 18, we sailed from Pearl Harbor to Saipan, our staging area. There we transferred to a smaller ship, an LST, and during the second week in February we participated in a final invasion rehearsal. We were now part of an armada that covered a vast stretch of the sea. On D-minus-4 we weighed anchor and started for Iwo Jima.

We had a pleasant voyage to the objective. The weather was balmy and we spent most of our time lounging around on deck waiting for chow call. There was little anxiety about the impending battle, since it hadn't yet taken on an aspect of reality. Though we were told the enemy might hit our shipping from the air, all we encountered was a single high-flying observation plane.

Our little LST was carrying many more men than she'd been designed for, and we assault troops had to sleep on deck. This pleased those of us who were subject to seasickness, for we needed all the fresh air we could get.

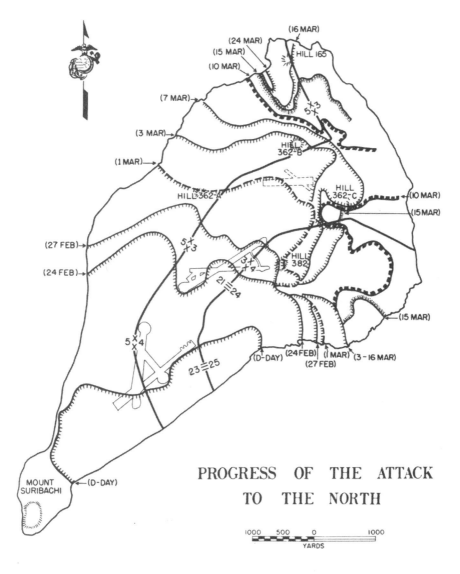

PROGRESS OF THE ATTACK

TO THE NORTH

On D-plus-9 (February 28) the 28th Marines got orders to join the 5th Division in its attack to the north. The division fought on the left. This map notes its progress to the end of the battle.

I had only one complaint during the three-and-a-half-day trip. The ship's head (toilet compartment) had been reserved for the crew and the officers among us. For the rest of us there had been placed on deck, near the port rail, a metal trough with two skimpy wooden seats. It was set at right angles to the rail, with an end extending out over the sea, and a continuous flow of water kept it flushed. The contraption was sanitary enough, but there was no screen around it. One had to sit there, his bare buttocks gleaming, before the eyes of half the men on deck. Perhaps not too many Marines minded being on display like this, but I had been raised in a household where the act of elimination was considered a strictly private affair. As a result the trough-toilet set me trying to regulate my bowels so my calls would come only during the hours of darkness.

WE HIT THE BEACH

As Iwo Jima's dawn gave way to full daylight we saw that D-day was starting fair. The island had been cloaked with mist during the bombardment of D-minus-1, but the sky had cleared during the night and visibility was now excellent. The temperature was in the high sixties. Only a mild wind was sweeping the ocean, and its surface held little more than ripples and light swells.

A quiet sea was vital to the invasion. Even under the best of conditions Iwo's surf was treacherous, since there was no harbor or protected area. The island's beaches sloped steeply and the waves came close to shore before breaking, and this made trouble for small craft operations.

Just a few hours before the arrival of our shipping the sea had been dangerously rough and had threatened to disrupt our landing schedule. But Iwo's waters were now about as gentle as they ever got. It seemed the gods of war were with us.

The seven-and-a-half-square-mile dot of land we were about to project into the news and elevate to lasting remembrance had been almost entirely unknown before World War II. Even the people of Japan, whose leaders had held dominion over Iwo for seventy years, were most of them unaware of its existence. It was located in the Nanpo Shoto, an island chain that began at the entrance of Tokyo Bay and extended in a southerly direction for about 750 miles.

Composed mainly of rocks, sand, sulphur and patches of scraggy subtropical vegetation, Iwo lacked natural sources of fresh water. Its occupants had to rely on cisterns that held rain water, distilled salt water and water provided by visiting tankers. Until a few months before D-day the island had been the home of about eleven hundred civilians who lived in typical one-story Japanese cottages and depended on a sulphur refinery, a sugar mill, small-scale agriculture and fishing for a livelihood. They had been evacuated because our invasion was expected.

Iwo Jima was geographically and economically insignificant, but because of the way the United States had pressed its island-hopping war against Japan the "rock" had acquired a major strategic importance. It held two completed airfields and one in the process of construction. We had to have these facilities in order to speed up, and make safer, our raids on the enemy's homeland. The heavy bombers that were based in the Mariana Islands had to travel about fifteen hundred miles without fighter escort to reach Japan, and plane and crew losses were heavy. Our capturing Iwo would cut the distance to Japan in half. Another reason the island had to be taken was to stop the enemy from using its airfields against us.

Japan had launched full-scale preparations for Iwo's defense about a year before our coming. A desperate attempt had been made to render the island impregnable. Its manpower had been greatly increased and the garrison had worked feverishly to complete an elaborate system of caves, tunnels, blockhouses, bunkers, mutually supporting pillboxes, gun emplacements, mortar pits, rocket pits, mine fields, antitank ditches and trenches. Camouflage had been employed with maximum effectiveness.

Mount Suribachi had been made a semi-independent defense sector. Its approaches had been studded with fortifications, and the natural caves that honeycombed its steep slopes had been enlarged and improved, some being provided with multiple entrances. The volcano's armament had been planned to include coast defense guns, artillery pieces, antiaircraft guns, stationary tanks, mortars, rocket launchers, demolitions, machine guns, rifles and hand grenades.

As our transports eased into the positions where we assault troops would disembark, the pre-H-hour naval attack was maintaining its intensity. The weapons of eight battleships, five cruisers and nine LCI rocket ships were in furious action, and tons of exploding shells were smashing at the island's defenses. Iwo Jima probably hadn't been rocked like this since the ancient day its volcano had last erupted.

I watched the show from the rail of our LST and couldn't help but wonder if there wasn't a possibility the island had been neutralized by the relentless bombardment it had undergone. It had been the target of the longest and fiercest softening-up given any objective of the Pacific war. For six months before D-day it had been bombed regularly by the Army's 7th Air Force and had been attacked intermittently by the Navy. And for the past three days the Navy had been pounding it steadily.

Iwo seemed much too small to have taken all this without losing most of its ability to resist. There was a good chance, I decided, that the battle might not be nearly so bitter as had been predicted by two of our top commanders, Vice Admiral Richmond Kelly Turner and Lieutenant General Holland M.

"Howlin' Mad" Smith. I had a vision of our fanning out from the beach and capturing the island after only a few skirmishes.

My squad leader and friend, Sergeant Howard M. Snyder, of Huntington Park, California, was standing beside me at the rail, and I told him what I'd been thinking. Snyder, an ex-raider with four campaigns to his credit, smiled at my optimism.

"Don't fool yourself," he said. "The way the Japs dig in, bombardments just shake them up a little." Then he added, "Maybe I'm crazy, but I'm looking forward to this fight. I think it will beat anything I've seen so far."

Buried Japanese tank doubling as a pillbox in Suribachi's base defenses.

Photo by Lou Lowery

I myself had never been under fire. Though I had joined the Marines "to see action" at the outbreak of the war, my guard duty assignments had kept me a noncombatant. This had made me complain repeatedly. But now that I was about to land on an enemy beach some eight thousand miles from home I began to wonder whether I wanted to see action as badly as I had believed. I was just six weeks past my twenty-third birthday, and it suddenly occurred to me that I might not get much older. My feelings can best be described by an anecdote I had heard earlier in the war:

At the close of a battle for a Japanese-held island a Marine was approached by a newspaper correspondent who opened his interview by asking, "What were your thoughts while you were getting ready to hit the beach?"

"Well, I thought of a lot of things, I guess," the Marine answered. "But uppermost in my mind was this question: 'What in hell am I doing *here?*'"

About 7:00 o'clock we donned our combat gear and descended the two ladders that led into the semi-darkness of our LST's tank deck. The vessel's bow doors had been opened and its ramp lowered to the water, and we could peer out of the hold as we might have from a cavern. As we climbed aboard our assigned amphibian tractors their motors began to set up an ear-numbing clatter, and exhaust fumes were shortly thickening our throats and burning our eyes.

In a score of practice debarkations we had entered our landing craft by going over the side of our transport and climbing down a net. Now, in the actual invasion, we were debarking in a way that was almost entirely unfamilar to us. But any serviceman will tell you that this was hardly an unusual thing to happen.

Soon the throbbing tractors began to move forward jerkily, one by one, toward the bright opening. Their tracks clanked and screeched on the deck. I occupied the fourth or fifth craft, along with some twenty others. We were on our feet and were loaded with packs, gas masks, canteens, helmets and an assortment of weapons and ammunition that made for a tight squeeze. Our tractor nosed up a little as it reached the ramp; then it plunged clumsily into the water, raising a splash and throwing us hard against one another. The craft rocked about heavily for a moment; then its motor accelerated and it churned clear of the launching area.

By 7:45 all units of our company were off the LST and were bobbing around in a sea that was now glimmering with warm sunlight.

With H-hour fast approaching, the bombardment had been stepped up. Additional rocket ships and a large group of mortar ships had joined the attack. All weapons crews were hammering their targets determinedly, and smoke and dust now hung over the beach in great white, yellow and gray clouds.

Our company was scheduled to land with the assault's twelfth wave. Since H-hour had been set for 9:00 o'clock and the waves would hit the beach at five-minute intervals, we would reach the island about 9:55.

In addition to rifle companies like ours, the D-day force included high-priority support units such as tank and artillery battalions, rocket sections, communications men, engineers, Seabees and medical teams. Also being readied for landing were vessels loaded with a great variety of equipment and supplies.

All units of the early waves were now off their transports. Hundreds of small craft, divided into slowly circling groups, awaited the signal to head for shore. The landing zone began near Mount. Suribachi, the objective's left flank, and extended northward for nearly two miles.

At 8:05 the naval gunfire was temporarily lifted and seventy-two carrier-based bombers and fighter planes thundered to the attack. They showered rockets, bombs and machine gun bullets on Suribachi and on the beach and the rugged high ground that overlooked it from the right. Then forty-eight additional fighters, including twenty-four Marine Corsairs, flashed in and hit the same areas with fiery napalm bombs and more rockets and machine gun bullets.

During these strikes the gunfire support ships glided closer to the island. And as soon as the last planes withdrew they opened up with renewed fury.

At 8:30 an array of rocket ships that were armed also with 40-millimeter guns began to move toward the beach. They dispatched a hail of missiles, then veered off to the flanks to make way for the first wave of the assault. Nearly seventy armored amphibian tractors were now heading shoreward. They carried no troops but were mounted with 75-millimeter pack howitzers and machine guns. It was their mission to take up positions on the beach and provide cover for the landing of the waves of troop-carrying craft that were beginning to follow at 250-yard intervals.

At this point, fifteen heavy bombers from the Marianas droned over the island and added their powerful bombs to the Navy's deluge of shells and rockets. Another thirty bombers had been assigned to the strike but had been delayed or diverted because of bad weather between the Marianas and Iwo.

At 8:57, a few minutes before the armored tractors were due to reach the island, the naval gunners lifted their landing-zone fire and began to train their weapons on inland targets. During this interval the Marine Corsairs returned to strafe the beach. They roared in from the south past Suribachi, dropped close to shore as they fired, then peeled off over the sea. Additional runs were made five hundred yards inland.

The armored tractors climbed out of the water at 9:02. They had been firing busily on the way in, but now they were hindered by a sandy terrace that ran parallel to the water's edge and ranged up to fifteen feet in height. Many found it necessary to retreat into the surf to resume an effective fire.

At 9:05 the first wave of troop-carrying tractors hit the beach. The ramps at the rear of the vessels rattled down, and within moments there were hundreds of Marines spread along the 3,500-yard landing zone. These men found Iwo's gray volcanic sand loose and irregular and difficult to walk on.

In the air above Suribachi, one of our planes caught a burst of antiaircraft fire. The pilot died as the plane, trailing smoke, crashed into the sea between the fourth and fifth waves of landing craft.

Resistance to the invasion was light at first. Our early waves took only a few shells and some scattered small-arms fire. Since the enemy had anticipated our naval bombardment, the landing zone itself wasn't heavily manned. But it could be covered at every spot by inland emplacements. And by the time the fifth wave landed at 9:20, some of these were beginning to react energetically.

The wave that we of Easy Company were part of was at this point crossing the line of departure and was still a half hour's trip from the island. We forty-six men of the 3rd Platoon were crowded into two tractors, one group being led by Lieutenant Wells and the other by Platoon Sergeant Thomas.

While trying to keep our balance as we bobbed and swayed along, we couldn't help but jostle one another. Usually discomfort like this made us grumble, but at present our minds were busy with far graver concerns. I even forgot to think about seasickness. Often within a short time after I boarded a landing craft I was vomiting into my helmet shell, but this morning my helmet was intact and on my head. Though this may have been due partly to the mildness of the sea, the tenseness of the moment probably had a lot more to do with it.

The roar of the tractor's engine vibrated through its metal hull, drowning out the din of the action and impeding conversation. I was barely able to hear the man on my right when he said anxiously, "If only we get in okay!"

This same thought, of course, had occurred to me. I had prepared for the possibility of our craft getting hit and sunk by opening my cartridge belt so I could shed my cumbersome pack quickly. But I was trying to shut out the fear, and I hated to hear it spoken. "We'll get in okay!" I hollered back.

It is commonly believed that a group sharing a hazardous experience can find a certain strength in talking freely of their fears. But this belief isn't based on reality. Such talk can serve no purpose but to promote panic.

When we were nearing a position about halfway to the beach we passed close by the bow of the battleship *Tennessee*. Viewed from our tiny craft, hardly more than a cork on the water, the ship looked amazingly huge. Its gray plating rose beside us like a cliff and we had to bend our heads far back to see its decks. Its big guns were in action and their metallic booming penetrated the noise of our tractor. A group of sailors standing along one of the rails gestured and shouted at us. We couldn't hear them but we had a feeling they were saying something like, "Go get 'em, you damned glory hounds!" One of the men was drinking from a cup that very probably held hot coffee, and this sight seemed inconsistent with matters at hand.

Ernest Thomas, our group's leader, now turned his attention to the island. He had been standing close to the tractor's port gunwale, which was about chest-high, and he hoisted himself up until he was sitting on the gunwale and could peer past the port gun shield. The rest of us continued to keep our heads down.

Up to this time the landing operation as a whole was going well. Bullets were pecking at numerous craft, and shells were menacing others, but only a few had been put out of commission. One, however, had received a direct artillery hit and had gone down fast, taking several men with it. The rest of the men were pulled from the water by occupants of nearby vessels.

We were still some distance from the island when Mount Suribachi, craggy and forbidding, began to loom up on our left-front. We would beach on the landing zone's extreme left flank, only a few hundred yards from the volcano's base. I hunched lower in the tractor as it occurred to me that high-positioned snipers might already have us in their sights. Corporal Robert Leader, who was stationed at our craft's starboard gun, heard a *ping-ping-ping* of machine gun fire across its shield. This burst had passed close over our coxswain's head.

The harsh odor of cordite was beginning to reach us. It was being borne out over the water by an eight or ten knot wind that was moving across the island from the north.

Group of Fifth Division Marines on way to beach.

Photo by Lou Lowery

Just before we gained shore a heavy booming again got through our tractor's racket, and some of us thought we were meeting an enemy gun head on.

"It's one of our own! It's one of our own!" Ernest Thomas shouted. And a moment later we saw this for ourselves. As our craft's tracks touched bottom we passed one of the armored tractors of the first wave. Its pack howitzer was striking toward the left at a target on Suribachi.

Our craft climbed out of the surf and came to a stop. We were "in."

THE ISLAND GETS HOT

As the ramp at the rear of the tractor started to drop, Ernest Thomas yelled to me: "Wheeler, you and Adrian unload the supplies!" He was referring to the seven hundred pounds of mortar shells, small-arms ammunition, rations and water our craft was carrying.

I grabbed Pfc. Louie Adrian by the arm as the men began to scramble out. Adrian was a tall, fine-looking Spokane Indian from Wellpinit, Washington. He and I, working at top speed with our rifles slung and both hands free, started to toss the crates and cans over the side and onto the wet sand. The task took us only about a minute, but the tractor's coxswain, impatient to leave the island, was already retracting the ramp as we finished. Climbing its incline on the run, we leapt off its edge into a knee-deep breaker. We unslung our rifles as we circled to our left and started up the beach toward our squad.

With the tractor's engine no longer roaring in our ears, we became aware of the island's desperate medley of combat sounds. Guns were booming, shells were whining and crashing, machine guns and rifles were rattling and men were shouting. From overhead came the drone of aircraft.

One member of our platoon had already become a casualty. Pfc. Bert M. Freedman, our Hawaiian Islander, was sitting at the water's edge gripping an ankle, and a Navy hospital corpsman was hurrying to his side. Freedman had taken a bullet in the foot as he cleared the tractor. Though he was frowning as though in pain, he seemed almost a man to envy. His early wound meant evacuation and survival.

As the Indian and I moved up the beach we anxiously scanned Mount Suribachi to our left and the sand that rose in terraces before us. The sand was friendly with Marines, but Suribachi, with its brushy approaches, its ashen dome, its fissures and its shadows, was an ominous sight. Though scattered patches of smoke told us the volcano was still being shelled by the Navy, there were also many spots where gun muzzles flashed in retaliation.

On discovering that there were no enemy troops in the open, Adrian asked, "Where's the reception committee?"

He apparently expected a lot of the island's defenders to be swarming from their caves, bunkers, pillboxes and other fortifications in an attempt to hurl us back into the sea. But exposed Japanese would be an infrequent sight on Iwo. Our adversaries would do most of their fighting from their labyrinth of defenses. A few counterattacks would be launched, but the traditional *banzai* attack had been banned because it was too costly a measure. Iwo's top officer, Lieutenant General Tadamichi Kuribayashi, knew he could hold the island longer if the majority of his men fought from cover until they were destroyed.

General Kuribayashi was much respected by his countrymen for his capability and his fighting spirit. He had reported to Iwo eight months before, directly from Tokyo where he had been commanding the 1st Imperial Guards Division, the unit responsible for the security of the Imperial Palace. While so serving he had been accorded the singular honor of an audience with Emperor Hirohito.

Early moments of the D-day landing of the 5th Division about a half-mile from Mount Suribachi.

Defense Dept. Photo

It was largely through Kuribayashi's efforts that Iwo had acquired its phenomenal defensive strength. But, in one of his letters to his wife in Tokyo, the general had written sadly that he knew he had come to the island to die. He realized that American forces would ultimately overrun his own. But he felt that Iwo had to be defended to the last man so that the assault on Japan itself might be delayed as long as possible.

The group Adrian and I landed with had moved in from the water a short distance and dropped into prone positions on the sand. We two found a space between Howard Snyder, our squad leader, and Pfc. John J. Fredotovich, a raven-haired college student from Oakland, California.

Adrian, Fredotovich and I were the men of Snyder's first fire team. Fredotovich was the team's BAR man (Browning automatic rifleman), while Adrian and I were armed with eight-shot Garands. Being a corporal, I was the little unit's leader. I was also Snyder's assistant squad leader.

Our platoon's other tractor had reached shore about fifty yards to our right. The craft had been unable to climb out of the surf because of troop congestion at the water's edge, and Lieutenant Wells had been obliged to order his men over the side. They had landed in waist-deep water and had lost some of their extra equipment. But they were now moving up on our right flank. One of the first things that had caught their attention was an unattached leg that was trickling blood into the sand. It was bare except for a gray-and-white sock and a brown field shoe, items that told them the limb had belonged to a fellow Marine and not to a Japanese.

The island's first terrace-front sloped up a few yards ahead of our location. It was crowded with Marines of the waves that had landed just before our own. These men—members of the 2nd Battalion, like ourselves—were awaiting the outcome of a lunge across the island being made by the 1st Battalion units that had led our regiment's landing. It was the 1st Battalion's hazardous mission to push to the western beach as fast as possible and isolate Mount Suribachi.

Our own platoon's initial orders called for us to make our way to a preselected area where the units of our company would assemble to reorganize. This maneuver would carry us roughly 350 yards. We would move about two hundred yards along the beach to our right, away from Suribachi, and then would head about 150 yards inland.

Iwo was only seven hundred yards wide in our zone. About half the distance was barren sand, while the remainder held a sparse covering of scrubby trees and brush. There were few defenses in the open stretch, but the scrubwood had been strongly fortified. It was now crackling with small-arms fire and resounding with heavier explosions, and we knew the 1st Battalion was meeting stiff opposition.

Our company was to follow these men, when it became practicable, and occupy the ground they had captured. The other two companies of the 2nd Battalion were to string their lines across the island, facing Suribachi, in preparation for our regiment's main attack. Our 3rd Battalion was in floating reserve.

It was imperative that Mount Suribachi be taken quickly. It served the Japanese not only as a fortress but as an observation post that commanded a view of two-thirds of the island. As long as the enemy held it, the movements of the bulk of our landing force could be clearly observed and the information could be relayed to the gun crews of widely scattered emplacements.

Due to the convexity of the terrain ahead of us we of the 3rd Platoon were screened from the fire of the fortifications the 1st Battalion was engaging. But we lay directly under the guns of Suribachi's northeastern defenses. Many of these were no longer undergoing naval attack because they were too close to our lines, and the enemy had begun to put them into effective operation. Artillery and mortar shells were whoomping along the beach, and small-arms fire was weaving an invisible criss-cross pattern just above it.

A stranger near my fire team took his entrenching shovel from his pack and began to scoop a hole in the sand. "You'd better start digging in," he hollered to us. "You've got to keep busy or you'll go nuts!"

There was a note of hysteria in the man's voice, and it troubled me in the same way as had the anxious words of my companion in the tractor. The stranger's advice was sound, however, and I considered taking it until I saw that ex-raider Snyder wasn't reaching for his entrenching tool. I didn't want to appear more concerned about concealment than he. Adrian and Fredotovich made no move to dig either.

A few minutes later Fredotovich, who was lying beside me with his right shoulder almost touching my left, fell victim to a mortar shell. The thumping explosion, accompanied by a wave of concussion and a spray of sand, occurred very close to his left side. He received two serious wounds. One fragment smashed into his ribs near his shoulder blade and another cut deep into his upper leg.

Rising to my knees, I shouted for a corpsman and began to fumble for the small first aid kit at the wounded man's belt. The spots where his clothing had been torn by the fragments were rapidly saturating with blood. Chilled by this sight, I realized how close I myself had been to disaster. The shell had landed little more than the breadth of Fredotovich's body from my position. The unfortunate man, in fact, had served me as a shield.

"I'm going ... I'm going ..." Fredotovich said in low calm tones.

While I fed him his sulfa tablets with a swallow of water from one of his canteens I assured him that the only place he was going was back to a nice clean bunk on a hospital ship. Then I added, "You're getting out of here before things really get rough." The remark was a foolish one. For Fredotovich, things were already about as rough as they could be.

"Get his BAR," Snyder ordered.

Kuribayashi supervising the island's buildup.

Photo provided by the general's widow

I passed the weapon to Adrian. He placed it on the sand and helped me to ease the belt of ammunition from the wounded man's middle.

"You'd better get his watch, too," Snyder said. "We might need it."

I was about to object to this, since the watch wasn't government property, when a corpsman arrived and yelled, "Leave this man alone—he's badly hurt!" I was glad to obey.

Fredotovich's plight was especially lamentable because he might have missed out on the invasion except for his strong sense of duty. A few weeks before we left California for Hawaii he had injured a ligament in his knee during a field problem and had been sent to the base hospital. The leg had not yet healed when he got word that we would soon ship out. He had managed to get himself released and had limped back to duty just a few days before we left.

Snyder now told the Indian to discard his Garand and take up the wounded man's BAR. Our platoon's automatic rifles were a vital part of its fire power. They held 20-round clips and were equipped with bipods for prone firing.

It was time for us to start working our way toward our company rendezvous area, and our lieutenant got to his feet and shouted above the din, "Let's move out!" He took off along the terrace to the right, his Thompson submachine gun swinging in his hand.

Reluctantly rising from our indentations in the sand, we began to follow. We felt suddenly very conspicuous and expected momentarily to find our flesh yielding to a bullet or a piece of jagged steel. The dreaded projectile, we knew, might even come from directly underfoot. We had been told the beach was very probably mined.

Anxiety had by this time attached a heavy weight to the inside of my breastbone. Though I had naturally expected combat to be perilous I hadn't fully realized how concentrated this battle would be. My impressions of warfare had been shaped chiefly by books and moving pictures that dealt with battles involving great areas and including spots where participating units could feel relatively safe.

When all the troops of our assault were ashore Iwo Jima would be the most heavily populated seven and a half square miles on earth. There would be precious little room for maneuvering, and almost every foot we occupied could be reached by enemy guns. Units in reserve would at first be obliged to dig in just a few yards behind front-line troops, and they would be apt to take almost as much fire. There would be times when they would take even more. Conversely, when a unit was relieved of forward duty it would be likely to find its retirement area very much like the front. This situation would be responsible for a nervous strain of such continuance as to be unique in warfare.

Each of us wouldn't, of course, be under fire at every moment. There would be many lulls in the enemy's resistance as far as our individual units were concerned. But even during these lulls we would know we were within easy range of a host of guns. And we would realize that we could hardly make a move that escaped Japanese notice. We troops in the Suribachi area would be particularly conscious of this. We would seldom be more than a half mile from the volcano, and much of the time we would be plainly exposed to the view of observers, gun crews and riflemen in the caves on its slopes and at its summit. Even when we were in holes we wouldn't feel undetectable, however low we pressed our-selves. This sensation of being watched over gunsights by hundreds of hostile eyes would be very nearly as unnerving as being actually under fire.

The loose sand was hard to negotiate. We wanted to run, in obedience to our training and our instincts, but, loaded with gear as we were, we could only plod. We divided the trip into short jumps, stopping frequently to hit the sand so we wouldn't remain conspicuous for too long at a time.

Our route was crowded with Marines. Some were lying prone or were dig-ging in, while others were climbing the terrace-front and moving inland. Troop congestion was mounting dangerously. We were all aware of the importance of dispersion in combat, but our zone's narrow confines prevented us from keeping sufficiently spaced.

Litter begins to accumulate at shoreline, the result of hostile gunfire, a treacherous surf and yielding sand.

Defense Dept. Photo

We passed a number of tallow-faced casualties who were being treated by corpsmen, and we saw a blinded man being led to the water's edge for evacuation. The latter had a hand clasped to a bandage over his eyes, and there was blood on his cheeks. He was stumbling every few steps because of irregularities in the sand.

We moved around one figure that was completely covered with a poncho and was lying very still. This somber form only minutes before had been a vigorous young man who had been accepted into the Marine Corps because of his hale physique, his sharp vision and hearing, his sound teeth.

The sight of death probably impresses everyone a little differently. I would think of each dead Marine I saw on Iwo Jima largely in terms of his teeth. "Another fine set of teeth going to the grave," I would lament to myself. From earliest youth I had been teeth-conscious, and I knew so many Marines whose beautiful teeth gave them smiles that seemed to embody their bright young personalities. I considered the world decidedly sadder for each of these smiles it lost.

It occurs to me now that the teeth of these interred Marines are still sound. By this time the flesh of their skulls has moldered and they are smiling again. Since a man's smile is the last part of him to decay, perhaps some of the very same smiles I admired so much will be marveled at by archeologists a thousand years hence.

Our attention was once drawn to a landing craft that was approaching the beach. It was an LCVP, a vessel that held perhaps twice as many men as an amphibian tractor and had its ramp at its forward end. The craft had a large American flag secured to one of its gunwales, a bold gesture on the part of its occupants, since they must have known the flag would invite a concentration of enemy fire. The Marines were carrying their display of defiance to the limit, for they were shouting lustily as their vessel cut through the surf and thrust its prow against the shore. Then as the ramp dropped to the sand and the men bolted out they took a direct artillery hit, and their spirited shouts were instantly replaced by cries of anguish and confusion.

Another appalling sight shortly presented itself. About a hundred yards to our left-front a Marine was blown high into the air. Looking like a great rag doll, he went up end over end and seemed to rise at least fifty feet before plummeting back to the sand. A heavy caliber shell had apparently burrowed directly under him before exploding.

During one of our stops we drew fire from a totally unexpected source. There was a wrecked enemy ship lying offshore, and a number of snipers and observers were lurking in it. The shots directed at us were ineffective, but they made us start moving again in a hurry.

Private John G. Scheperle, one of our Missourians, had his BAR torn from his hands by machine gun fire from the volcano. He wasn't hit, but his weapon was damaged. Lieutenant Wells told him to keep his eyes open for a good BAR that had been laid aside.

Several of our men once took cover against the terrace-front at a spot where it was about six feet high and sharply inclined. A few moments later our Massachusetts art student, Robert Leader, suddenly found himself completely buried. An artillery shell had exploded in the sand above his head and had moved a portion of the terrace over him. Two of his friends leapt to his aid. Somewhat confused as to what had happened, Leader felt himself being uncovered, pulled free and dusted off roughly, and he heard one of his rescuers ask, "Are you all right?" He was relieved to be able to reply that he was.

Some of our men scratched out hurried foxholes each time we hit the sand. Pfc. Leo Rozek, of Muskegon, Michigan, found this a dangerous thing to do. He was once busily scooping away the sand with his hands when he felt his fingers strike a metallic object, and he discovered to his horror that he was clawing at the side of a land mine. Moving quickly to another spot, he started to dig again, and, incredibly enough, he uncovered a *second* mine. He was more fortunate with his third try.

At length completing the first leg of our move, we found an area that was comparatively free of congestion and stopped for an extended breather. Some of the men dropped into handy depressions, some began to dig foxholes, and some settled against the terrace-front, which here was about five feet high. I did the last.

Near me was Corporal Charles W. "Chuck" Lindberg, of Minneapolis, Minnesota, a former raider who led our assault squad and was also one of its flame-thrower men. He was square-set and muscular, with good features, and he had a jovial rough-and-ready manner that we liked. There was half a finger missing from his left hand, and we had often reminded him, during our field problems, that he was especially endowed for the range-indicating we had to do with our fingers. (When we estimated the distance to a target and wanted to relay the information to a fellow platoon member without breaking silence we held up one finger for each hundred yards of our estimate.) We had enjoyed telling Lindberg, who took his impairment lightly, that he was the only man in the platoon who could indicate ranges in 50-yard units.

The ex-raider had an enviable combat record, and I had often complained to him about my own noncombatant status. Now as we sat against the terrace-front amid a growing storm of action I said, "Well, it looks as though I finally rate my first battle star."

Easing the 72-pound napalm rig from his shoulders, he answered, "You'd better wait and see if you get off this rock in one piece."

Then he turned and lay on his stomach against the sandy slope and pushed himself upward until he could peer toward the center of the island. He had barely got his eyes above the terrace before a mortar shell exploded a few feet in front of his head. He escaped injury from the blast of steel and sand, but a fragment put a nick in his helmet. Recoiling back down the slope, he took the helmet from his head and observed the nick. Then, fingering it and grinning uneasily, he looked at me and said, "See what I mean?"

Corporal Leonce "Frenchy" Olivier, of Eunice, Louisiana, a regimental headquarters man who had once been a member of the 3rd Platoon, had occasion to pass through our area a short time later, and he stopped for a few minutes near my position. Olivier was probably the only Marine who landed on Iwo Jima with a 1903 Springfield rifle instead of the newer Garand that was now the corps' standard weapon. He had used a Springfield on Tarawa, and he grumbled when he was issued a Garand during his training with the 5th Division. I had heard him say several times that he would have a Springfield when we went into action, and he had somehow managed to fulfil his boast.

"This is going to be worse than Tarawa," Olivier told me. He had won the Silver Star for his part in that shockingly bloody assault, and I figured he might

Unloading of supplies as seen from the bow of a vessel rammed up on shore.

Marine Corps Photo

very well know what he was talking about. But I wasn't at all pleased to hear the prediction.

The strain of being under fire was already beginning to show on the faces of most members of our platoon. Some displayed a definite anxiety, their brows being drawn into a deep frown. Others had a kind of round-eyed blank look. It was as though their facial muscles had gone numb.

Our new area presently became warm. Two larger-type landing vessels (LSMs) pushed their prows up on the beach near us to unload their cargoes through their bow doors, and they promptly drew artillery fire. Crashing shells began to raise waterspouts in the shallows about them. Most of the shrapnel that came in our direction whirred well over our heads, but I shortly heard a stray fragment thud into the terrace-front. I huddled lower and began to wish I had dug in. I was still following ex-raider Snyder's example, and he had so far made no particular effort to conceal himself.

Our lieutenant was on his feet when the shelling began, and he turned to watch it without ducking. But one of our combat veterans quickly rose and yanked him down. And this unceremonious act saved Wells from injury or death, for a huge fragment sped over him as he hit the sand.

During these tense moments, Pfc. Richard S. White, a sandy-haired Texan who was dug in about fifty feet from me, cupped his hands to his mouth and shouted in my direction, "Hey, Wheeler! Are you still an atheist?"

"I'm going to start to pray any minute!" I yelled back.

My friends considered me an atheist because I had written and circulated several irreverent little poems during our training period. I can remember only one of these. It was entitled "The Afterlife" and went as follows: "When I leave my tomb/On the Day of Doom/I will shun the celestial place./I intend to dwell/In eternal hell/With the rest of the human race."

But in spite of my fondness for impious sentiments I wasn't an atheist. I was only a skeptic. And I did do some praying on Iwo. My prayers were unorthodox, being addressed to "whatever gods may be," but they were prayers nonetheless.

There was soon a lull in the artillery fire, and our platoon began its next move. Climbing the terrace-front, we struggled up the barren incline toward the center of the island. We must have presented clear targets to the Japanese on the volcano, but only a few bullets snapped through our ranks and we were able to keep going.

We saw a radioman of another unit do a kind of toe dance when machine gun fire started to spatter around his feet. He couldn't run because of the weight of his equipment but seemed to think he could avoid the bullets by keeping his feet in motion. Whatever the worth of his footwork, he did manage to move out of the line of fire without being hit.

One of the shell holes we passed held a group of crouching men that included a chaplain whose white face indicated he wasn't at all certain, at this point, that he was being looked after by the Almighty. It semed strange to see a frightened chaplain, but his fright was normal enough. Believers and nonbelievers alike were being maimed and killed. About the only advantage the believers had over the nonbelievers was the feeling they were endowed with eternal life. But maybe not many of them had even this advantage. Few men have a faith strong enough to exclude all doubt about the hereafter when death is looming. Perhaps almost everyone in our landing force, from chaplain to atheist, was worried about the possibility of everything ending for him right there on Iwo's gray sand. Perhaps almost everyone was troubled by the look of absolute finality about those bodies that had been wrapped in ponchos and were awaiting burial.

We didn't stop and take cover until we had reached our company rendezvous area, a stretch of sand that lay well above the level of the beach. Our commanding officer, Captain Dave Severance, and numerous other men of the company were already there.

RINGED BY FURY

We stayed in the rendezvous area, waiting the order to follow the 1st Battalion across the island, until perhaps 1:00 P.M. Our situation was exceptional. We were surrounded by violence but were not much affected by it. Little enemy fire came our way, even though the sand we clung to was plainly visible to Mount Suribachi.

The volcano-fortress, with its glowering 550-foot dome, stood about a half mile to our left, and we saw it for the first time from the angle from which it would have to be assaulted. Though its farther sides dropped to meet the sea, the side facing us was semi-circled by brush-covered approaches that held a 1,300-yard belt of blockhouses, bunkers, pillboxes, mortar pits, tunnels, trenches and other defenses. These would prove to be the volcano's real strength. The caves in its dome were formidable, some being big enough to hold scores of men, but many would serve the enemy as dismal deathtraps rather than as potent fortifications. Because of the camouflage that had been employed from approaches to summit, we could see nothing of the elaborate defense setup but the dark shadows of a few cave entrances and the jagged concrete walls of several blockhouses that had been blasted by the Navy. The fortress was still taking shellfire that was raising puffs of smoke, volcanic ash, pulverized rock, splintered brush and other debris.

About a third of the way between our location and Suribachi, Companies D and F of the 2nd Battalion were struggling over the open terrain, against mounting opposition, to get on line across the island. Their attack on the volcano was scheduled to start at 3:45 that afternoon. Shells were spewing up sand among these men, and the occasional ricocheting bullets that whined over our heads told us they were also taking machine gun and rifle fire. Fortunately the area held an abundance of shell holes and bomb craters, and the units were able to take cover between advances.

This suggests an interesting thought regarding the preliminary work of the Navy and the 7th Air Force. Even those shells and bombs that landed ineffectively on the sand were important to the success of the invasion. Some of the pits were six or eight feet deep and were large enough in diameter to hold several men. Many Marines doubtless escaped death or injury because of this ready cover.

Ahead of our position about 150 yards was the scrubwood through which the 1st Battalion was pressing its noisy and costly attack toward the opposite shore. Two platoons—or, more fittingly, the remnants of two platoons—had managed to make it across by 10:30, just ninety minutes after H-hour. These men had rammed through a host of bunkers, pillboxes and machine gun nests. They had silenced some of the defenses with small-arms fire, flame throwers, demolitions and hand grenades, but they had bypassed many others, leaving them to be reduced by platoons that were following.

Because of the suicidal nature of its mission, the 1st Battalion was sustaining casualties that would exceed those of any other battalion on the island the first day. And the unit's companies were becoming badly disorganized. They had been expected, after completing the crossing, to swing to the left and join the 2nd Battalion in its Suribachi attack. But it was fast becoming clear that our regiment's reserve battalion, which was still afloat, would have to be committed against the volcano in the 1st Battalion's stead.

One of the men who had landed with the 1st Battalion was a friend of mine, a husky bronze-faced sergeant I had served with in Alaska. He was profane, audacious and mischief-loving, and during our Alaskan tour he had drunk lustily, brawled because he found it fun, and regularly patronized "Maude's Place," a brothel near our base. He'd had the unique experience of having one of the girls fall in love with him. She was the most sought-after girl in the house and was surprisingly pretty. Most of the time she belonged to men in general, but on my friend's days off she forsook all others to become his alone. He seemed to regard her with a certain fondness, but his basic attitude toward the relationship was aptly illustrated by a sentence he used to describe her: "She's not much bigger than my fist, but she's a damned sight better!"

Through my friend, I myself had a brief encounter with Maude's Place. One evening while he was on duty as a military policeman he took me along on one of his hourly inspections of the establishment. I found it to be a one-story frame building with a central hallway that had perhaps a half dozen rooms along either side. A moment after we entered, one of the nearer doors opened and a stocky middle-aged woman looked out.

"Oh, it's you again, Harry," she said, breaking into a smile that was friendly but somewhat lacking in teeth.

"Yep!" my friend answered. Then, to my surprise and discomfort he announced, "Look, Maude—I've brought you a virgin!"

The madam frowned. She said firmly, "I don't like virgins!" And she forthwith closed the door.

I paid no more visits to Maude's Place.

Upon our returning to the States the sergeant and I had both been assigned to the 28th Marines. But, being in different battalions, we saw little of each other during our training in California and Hawaii. Then, a few weeks before our regiment boarded ship to head for action, Harry had looked me up to tell me he'd managed to learn some classified intelligence. Our objective, he informed me, would definitely be Iwo Jima. Furthermore he said he knew that his company would land with the first wave of the assault.

At the time I felt this information might be just another scrap of scuttlebutt, but I didn't say so. In fact I told him, in my ignorance of what lay ahead, that I envied him and his outfit the distinction of having been picked to spearhead our regiment's attack. He had responded with, "I wish to hell I could trade places with you!" And his anxiety about his position had been well founded, for the big, likeable hellion was among those who died in the 1st Battalion's valiant charge across the island.

There were many examples of individual heroism during the crossing. One man, Corporal Tony Stein, of Company A, earned the Congressional Medal of Honor. Stein, a handsome dark-haired youth, was armed with a "stinger," an air-cooled machine gun that had been taken from a wrecked Navy fighter plane in the Hawiian Islands. He exposed himself defiantly to deliver torrents of covering fire for his unit's advance. Each time his ammunition ran out he stripped off his encumbering equipment (including his helmet and his shoes), found a wounded comrade and helped him back to the beach, grabbed more ammunition and returned on the run to the front. He did this eight times. He also singlehandedly attacked several pillboxes and in this way accounted for at least twenty of the enemy. His energetic daring contributed vitally to the crossing's success.

Our view to the right was limited by a rise in the terrain, but over there another 5th Division regiment, the 27th, was infiltrating across the southern end of Airfield Number One. And still farther to the north two 4th Division regiments, the 23rd and the 25th, were pushing their way inland. All units were encountering strong resistance, and the island was a rumble of detonations.

It would be in the north, where Iwo's greater land area lay, that the main fighting would be done. The contest for Mount Suribachi, though highly important, would be only a small part of the battle.

Our supporting aircraft were keeping busy overhead. Some circled about, spotting and observing, while others struck in wrathful groups at Suribachi and at targets in the north. When they dived with gunned engines and sent their rockets, bombs and bullets slamming home, these planes were the loudest part of the attack.

Spread over the ocean behind us were the silver forms of countless ships. The array was an imposing picture of strength. Closer to the island, the water was dotted with smaller craft that were leaving long white wakes as they traveled to and from the beach.

Resistance to our landing activities had increased since we of the 3rd Platoon had come ashore. Our battalion had slipped in while the Japanese were still partly stunned by the pre-H-hour bombardment, but they had now made a strong recovery. The beach was receiving steady artillery and mortar fire, and a great chain of destruction was being forged at the water's edge. Useless landing vessels, cranes, trucks, jeeps and other pieces of equipment were settling haphazardly into the surf-soaked sand. But even more dispiriting was the landing zone's growing number of torn and bleeding bodies.

The wounded were being cared for in hastily organized aid stations, and, when conditions permitted, were being evacuated to hospital ships. None of the aid stations were immune to shellbursts, and some of the wounded were being hit a second time, sometimes fatally, while waiting evacuation. Medical personnel, too, were becoming casualties.

Hostile fire wasn't the only cause of the rapidly mounting congestion at the water line. As jeeps and trucks emerged from their landing craft they often

To escape retaliation, these rocketeers will hasten to another spot as soon as this round of firing ends.

Marine Corps Photo

bogged down in the soft sand before they cleared the ramp. Unless a tractor was on hand to tow a bogged vehicle free at once, the craft, its bow pinned to the beach, usually broached and swamped.

One of the enemy's most decisive blows was struck against our regimental rocket section. As the four truck-mounted launchers rolled from their vessels they were subjected to artillery fire, and three were quickly blasted out of commission. The one that remained, however, was able to go into action, and a ripple it fired into the slopes of the volcano caused a tremendous explosion. This prompted the shell-weary men on the beach, who assumed that an enemy ammunition dump had been demolished, to raise a loud cheer.

Our regiment's tank support, Company C, 5th Tank Battalion, was luckier than the rocket unit. Fourteen Shermans, two flame tanks, one tankdozer and one retriever landed at 11:30 on a stretch of beach about five hundred yards to our right. Though the operation was heavily shelled and was threatened also by congestion and a steep, soft terrace-front, only one tank was lost on the beach. These important machines had been ordered to proceed directly to the

Tank and amphibian tractors blasted by Japanese artillery. Landing-force shipping visible in rear.

Defense Dept. Photo

1st Battalion area to assist against the scrubwood defenses, but the cumbrous column was having trouble finding a suitable route inland.

The landing of our regiment's 75-millimeter halftracks and 37-millimeter guns had resulted in the loss of two of the latter. Though the halftracks delivered their first fire from the water's edge, the 37s had been moved across the beach and toward inland positions almost immediately.

It hadn't been possible for our artillery support to land as early as hoped. This unit—the 3rd Battalion, 13th Marines—had sent reconnaissance parties ashore at 10:30, and they had found the preselected battery positions still in enemy hands. It would be 2:00 o'clock before the big weapons started coming in.

Shortly after noon our regiment's floating reserve, the 3rd Battalion, came ashore over the same section of beach we had used. This landing was strongly contested, and the unit suffered numerous casualties and lost some of its equipment. And the opposition continued as the men tried to start their advance across the sand to the right-flank position they had been ordered to occupy for the drive on Suribachi.

The situation on the beach this first day would seriously impede the landing of supplies. Only the highest priority items—such things as ammunition, communications equipment, medical equipment, rations and water—would be brought in. Shore party personnel would be unable to do much more than stack the stuff above the high-water mark.

Amphibian tractors, amphibian trucks and weasels would prove invaluable during this phase of the battle of supply. Instead of unloading on the beach, many of these vehicles would take their precious cargoes directly to the front lines. On the return trip they would often evacuate casualties. There would be times when they would come up against active defenses and their operators would suddenly find themselves involved in the fighting.

In spite of exploding shells, a treacherous surf, loose sand, congestion and a lot of confusion, the battle of supply would be won. Marine, Navy, Seabee, Coast Guard and Army groups, working together, would win it. Directing their efforts would be beach-masters who issued their orders with the aid of loud-speakers. Soon a complete ship-to-shore communications system would be set up, large areas of the troublesome sand would be leveled by armored bulldozers, landing stations that boasted cranes and trucks and Marston-matting roadways would be established, and supply dumps would begin to grow.

Few critical shortages would develop among attacking units. Most of the material would be mechanically transported, but when mechanical supply lines failed there would always be volunteers ready to carry urgently needed items to the front on foot.

THE BRISTLING SCRUBWOOD

As noon came and went, some of us in the 3rd Platoon felt that we ought to be thinking about food. It was now more than seven hours since we'd had breakfast aboard the LST. A few of us at length took K-rations from our packs, perhaps for the sole purpose of proving we weren't too scared to eat. We did little more than nibble at the food. I bit a chunk off my ration's fruit bar, but my throat was tense and dry and I could hardly swallow. With the help of water from one of my canteens I finally finished the bar, but I made no attempt to eat anything else.

I offered to share my ration with Louie Adrian, who hadn't opened one of his own, but the Indian admitted he wasn't hungry. He was frowningly absorbed in a study of the volcano. Doubtless he was remembering, like most of us, the briefing we had been given on its defenses while we were aboard the *Missoula* and was worried about attacking them across several hundred yards of open sand. Adrian had more reason for concern than he knew. In less than forty-eight hours his well-knit young body would be lying lifeless at Suribachi's base.

When he finally turned his attention from the volcano the Indian began checking the mechanism of his newly acquired BAR and discovered that its bolt stuck when he tried to work it. He handed the weapon to me and I field-stripped it and learned that it was already fouled with fine sand. Since I was carrying, in a breast pocket, an old shaving brush I planned to use on my own rifle, I was able to remedy the trouble. But sand-jamming would be a constant threat to the efficiency of our weapons. And after Adrian's experience I would practice extreme care with my Garand, being particular how I laid it down and giving it regular dustings with my brush.

I still wasn't occupying a foxhole. Howard Snyder chose merely to lie on the sand, and I was continuing to do as he did. By this time, however, I was asking myself anxiously, "When is this man going to start digging?" As it would turn out, I'd never see him dig. He would take advantage of natural cover and shell holes and enemy trenches when they were handy, but he would be otherwise quite casual about his security.

Though Snyder and I had known each other for the brief period of six months, we were close friends. He had been transferred to the 3rd Platoon from another unit of our regiment only at the start of the Hawaiian Island half of our training, but had become one of our most liked and respected members. Though he stood just five-feet-seven and was small-boned and spare, he had a calm competence about him that convinced us he would be a good man to follow. His combat record also impressed us. He had taken part in four engagements as one of Carlson's Raiders.

In civilian life Snyder had managed a five-and-ten-cent store, and he expected to return to this job when the war ended. He had married just a few weeks before our regiment left the States for Hawaii, and he took pride in showing us photographs of his pretty brunette bride. During an early period of our overseas training he had spent much of his spare time reading a book entitled something like *Making Marriage Succeed*. He had discussed many of the author's observations with Louie Adrian, John Fredotovich and me (who were single), and after finishing the book he had mailed it to his wife, who he was certain would find it as interesting as he had.

Snyder had stood beside me aboard our transport as D-day dawned and told me he was looking forward to the assault. His attitude had puzzled me, since I knew his chief interest in life was his new marriage. I felt it would have been more natural for him to be apprehensive about the possibility of never again seeing his bride. But this pessimistic thought apparently hadn't entered his head. His conduct since we landed had convinced me he'd meant what he said about the assault. He hadn't only remained cool but had maintained a bold curiosity about the action around us, even though the platoon as yet had no offensive obligations. His zest for combat was obviously stronger than his concern for his safety.

But I was made of a different stuff. In my imagination I was at every moment being personally aimed at by a concealed Japanese rifleman or gunner, and I itched to unlimber my shovel and burrow deep into the sand. I looked with envy at those members of the platoon who had dug themselves almost out of sight. Even a quick hand-scratched furrow would have been a great comfort. But I didn't want to lose face with my dauntless friend, so I decided to keep pretending I cared as little about cover as he.

There were, of course, other Marines on Iwo who did only a minimum of hiding. They included even our battalion commander, Lieutenant Colonel Chandler W. Johnson. This surprised me, particularly since the colonel had once, during a field problem that involved simulated combat conditions, reprimanded me for not taking full advantage of the cover the terrain afforded.

Our colonel was an interesting figure. An Annapolis graduate whose home was in Highland Park, Illinois, he was perhaps forty years old and was of medium height and heavy-set. Beyond his hearing, many of the men referred to him as "Jelly Belly Johnson." When he was in a good mood he had a mellow, fatherly look, but when he was angry—which was often—he came closer to resembling a bulldog. He was a rigid disciplinarian and kept us apprehensive about losing his favor. But on Iwo he quickly began to earn our esteem. He strode about unflinchingly, wearing nothing on his head but a fatigue cap and carrying no gear except a .45 caliber pistol that was thrust into his right hip pocket. When he stopped to consult with one of his subordinates he would often stand erect, gesturing and pointing authoritatively and making no effort to keep the enemy from learning he was a senior officer.

In view of the emphasis that combat training places on security, it would seem that men like Chandler Johnson and Howard Snyder must be regarded with disapproval. But their kind are vital to a battlefield effort. It's true that a combat team must be composed mainly of cautious men; wholesale heedlessness under fire would certainly bring the team to disaster. But there is also a need for an audacious minority. It's this minority that sets the pace for an attack. If everyone were to dig in deeply and move only when it was really necessary—which is all that duty requires—the team's efforts would lack vigor. There must be a scattering of men who neglect their safety and act with a daring initiative. Most of the tough feats that win the medals are performed by men like this. Though they are called damned fools by many of their more cautious comrades, they are nonetheless greatly admired. They do much for morale, since they seem entirely unafraid; and their cool aggressiveness sets a standard that the cautious, not wishing to be too far outdone, follow to the best of their ability. And that's how objectives are taken and battles are won.

Our platoon's attention was drawn once more to the terrain ahead when Captain Dave Severance at last gave Lieutenant Wells the order to move us out. The 1st Battalion had now crossed the island in force, and it was time for our company to start pushing into the scrubwood to occupy the captured ground—and, if necessary, fight to hold it.

As an observation plane wheeled overhead we began another plodding advance across the yielding sand. But this move soon attracted machine gun fire from the volcano. Rapid bursts started to snap about our feet, some of the bullets ricocheting away with a high-pitched buzz. We wasted no time finding cover.

Howard Snyder and I, who had been moving abreast, dived on our stomachs in a skimpy depression. But we shortly realized we were exposed on the side facing the gun, for a burst struck so close to our heads it splashed sand in our faces.

"You okay?" I asked Snyder.

"Yeah," he answered. "But let's get out of here!"

We scrambled for new positions, and this time I jumped into a shell hole. It was a very shallow one, and I had to bend low to be safe.

Presently I heard our lieutenant announce, from a sand pocket a few yards away, "I'm going to leave my pack and gas mask here, and you fellows had better do the same. We'll come back for the stuff later. Right now we've got to be able to move!"

This was an agreeable suggestion, but as I sat up to take off my pack another burst of machine gun bullets danced about me. I quickly ducked low again, and the pack straps I couldn't disengage from my cartridge belt in this cramped position I cut with my combat knife.

It was a relief to shed the pack and mask. Together they probably weighed no more than twenty pounds, but their bulk made them unwieldy. Our remaining gear consisted of more immediate necessities. My own trappings were a helmet, a rifle, a bayonet, two fragmentation grenades, one thermite grenade, a cartridge belt, a knife, two canteens and a first aid kit—still a good 25-pound load.

"Okay, let's go!" Wells soon ordered.

I held my breath as I rose, but nothing happened. The machine gun had either been silenced or had changed targets. We were able to step faster now, and a short time later we entered a hummocky area that gave us a little concealment.

While picking our way among the rises in a southwesterly direction we came upon a lone wounded Marine. He was lying on his back with his head resting on his folded poncho, and there was a blood-soaked bandage about his bared abdomen.

"Hey, Mac!" he called as I was going by. "Do you know whether there's a stretcher on the way for me?"

I hadn't seen any stretcher bearers since we'd left the beach, but I felt obliged to answer, "Yeah, I think there is."

I told this lie partly to ease the wounded man's mind and partly to avoid the possibility of having to deal with a request to go back and get help for him. We had been taught to leave the wounded to the medical teams. This seemingly forgotten Marine would probably soon be found by stretcher bearers who would take him to an aid station. That he hadn't been found already was undoubtedly due to the trouble our evacuation setup was being caused by the chaos on the beach.

We were soon in the open again and were now only about seventy-five yards from the scrubwood. Dead ahead of us stood one of the area's outlying fortifications. It appeared at first to be merely a large pile of sand, but the slope that faced us held a dark rectangular aperture that told us we were approaching a reinforced concrete gun emplacement. Its covering sand served both to camouflage it and to give it extra protection. We eyed the sinister-looking mound nervously but continued to move toward it. If it offered no resistance we would assume it had been reduced by the 1st Battalion and would cut around it into the scrubwood.

Then the black aperture began to spurt fire, and machine gun bullets once more whipped among us. We lunged for cover, some of us finding craters or depressions and others falling behind a foot-high terrace that extended part way across our path. Again all of us somehow escaped being hit.

Our lieutenant at this point came into contact with his first dead Japanese. The corpse was lying on its back in a shell hole and its abdominal organs had been laid bare by shrapnel. In his jump for concealment Wells landed on the man in such a way that his knees squashed into the exposed organs. He said later: "After that my pants legs smelled so bad that at one time I almost cut them off."

Since we had all taken the closest available cover, many of us were poorly shielded. We pressed ourselves as flat as possible, and our hearts pounded against the sand. Those of us who were seeing our first combat had suddenly learned what it meant to be pinned down by an enemy pillbox.

Up to this time our platoon had been fortunate. Since we had lost Bert Freedman and John Fredotovich on the beach we had covered five hundred dangerous yards without incurring another casualty. But now it seemed as though our run of good luck had ended.

We all knew how a rifle platoon was supposed to handle a problem like this. While one man semicircled his way to the pillbox with a demolitions charge, the rest were to deliver a concentrated fire at the aperture and make it impossible for the gun crew to operate. When the demolitions man was close enough to make a dash for the aperture and push his charge inside, the others were to cease firing—but only long enough for the man to make his play. The moment he turned away, the firing was to be resumed so the charge couldn't be expelled. We had executed this maneuver numerous times in training, using live rifle ammunition and actual charges of TNT. The importance of close support for the exposed attacker had been strongly emphasized. In the case of one of our regiment's platoons this had been overdone. A demolitions man was shot and killed in the act of placing his charge.

As we lay in our places of skimpy concealment and considered the obstacle before us, the prescribed method of dealing with pillboxes seemed suddenly unfeasible. Few of us felt like poking our heads up high enough to fire our rifles, and the idea of a man's rising and venturing across that barren sand seemed absurd. But if Wells gave the order the measure would be tried.

Then we heard a shell explode about fifty yards to our right. We looked in that direction in time to see another burst raise a tall jet of sand. Our first thought was that this fire was meant for us and would shortly be coming closer. Then we realized what the enemy was aiming at. Two beautiful olive-green Sherman tanks were clattering around our flank. The column of armor had at last been able to get through from the beach. Four machines had already been put out of commission by antitank fire, but the column was still strong and was now ready to help mop up the scrubwood. We were very happy to see the two leaders head straight for the pillbox that had us pinned down. With their 75-millimeter guns booming, the dynamic machines rolled into point-blank range. The reduction was soon accomplished. As the tanks ceased firing and started toward the scrubwood, the pillbox took on a tomblike stillness. And a tomb, of course, is what the structure had become.

We resumed our advance and shortly reached the first fringe of brush. There we received a gratifying surprise. The scrubwood's defenses included an extensive network of trenches and antitank ditches, and since the 1st Battalion had routed most of the Japanese from these excavations we would be able to use them for cover.

Falling into single file with Wells in the lead, we entered one of the roomy antitank ditches and began to thread our way toward the west coast. Our orders called for us to go all the way across. We would maintain our single-file formation, sticking as much as we could to the ditches and trenches, for the whole 400-yard trip. Our progress was slow, since we stopped often for extended periods while Wells and Ernest Thomas reconnoitered and made decisions as to the best route to follow.

We moved among numerous bunkers and pillboxes, some of which had been reduced and some of which appeared untouched but were quiet. All of the structures were well covered with sand. This gave some an almost-conic appearance, while others were closer to being igloo-shaped. The camouflaging effect of the sand was often enhanced by patches of grass and other low vegetation. Several of the mounds we saw were smoking as the result of flame thrower assaults, and we passed close by one whose interior was venting a fire-cracker-like series of snaps and pops as its ammunition supply exploded. Since the unassaulted structures didn't resist our advance we left them alone. They would be blown by men of the 5th Engineer Battalion, a unit that would aid our regiment importantly in its conquest of Suribachi.

There were groups of 1st Battalion wounded scattered through the antitank ditches. These men had been given first aid by their unit corpsmen and were waiting evacuation. Their position was most unenviable, since the area still held live Japanese. Some of the bandaged and bloodstained men were lying with their eyes closed, while others watched us pass. The watchers remained silent, and we did the same. I found myself disliking to pay the wounded too much attention. Thinking about them increased my awareness that I might at any moment be sharing their plight.

We saw few of the 1st Battalion's Japanese victims. There were several sprawled in open gun emplacements, but most were inside the assaulted bunkers and pillboxes. It's possible that some had fallen in the ditches and trenches but had been furtively dragged into concealment by their surviving comrades. This policy of Iwo's defenders would not only make it hard for us to estimate their remaining strength but would tug at our morale. For the first few days the battle would seem painfully one-sided. We would see many of our own casualties, but there would be little indication the Japanese were being destroyed in substantial numbers.

That the scrubwood still held live defenders was demonstrated to a group of us while we were moving through a waist-deep trench. There was an antitank ditch running parallel to the trench about fifty feet to our right, and we suddenly heard a jumble of excited Japanese voices coming from its depth. Our company executive officer, 1st Lieutenant Harold G. Schrier, was traveling with us at the time, and he quickly cautioned us to get down and be quiet. We dropped to our knees, tense and breathless, our weapons poised for action. But the voices shortly began to recede and in a few moments had faded entirely.

At one point Lieutenant Wells, while leading us into a shallow trough between two sand ridges, almost tripped a partly exposed mine. He had been studying the battered fuselage of a fallen Japanese plane up ahead, and he

Fighting in the scrubwood.

Defense Dept. Photo

noticed the mine just in time. Before going on he placed Ernest Thomas at the spot to guide us around it.

It was late afternoon when we approached the defense perimeter the 1st Battalion had set up along the high ground overlooking the western beach. Enemy shellfire had caused a gap to be left in the line, and it was this gap we were ordered to occupy. Happily the fire was lifting as we started moving in. The area held several of the now-familiar mounds that were bunkers and pillboxes.

At the base of one of the larger mounds lay two Marines who were dying of multiple bullet wounds. Their platoon leader, a young 2nd lieutenant, was sitting with them. Our own lieutenant's attention was drawn to the mound. It hadn't been reduced, and he realized it was big enough to hold an artillery piece. Its concrete doors were closed and it was altogether silent, but he felt that with night coming on it should be attended to without delay. He judged it to be a threat to the perimeter.

Deciding to blow the structure, he ordered Pfc. Clarence R. Hipp, of Brownwood, Texas, to ready a demolitions charge. If it was to be used, however, the two fatally wounded Marines would have to be moved. When Wells asked the young officer to have them carried away, an argument resulted. Wells, though, was the more persistent, and the officer finally summoned several of his men. The dying pair didn't complain when they were lifted, but there was anguish in their pallid faces.

Wells and Hipp now prepared to use the charge. But a 1st Battalion captain who had been walking along the perimeter and had heard the argument chose to interfere.

"Don't waste your charge on that one," he said. "I'm sure it's only a supply house. It's been quiet all day."

Our lieutenant was outranked this time, and the captain was determined that we bypass the mound. So we moved ahead about twenty-five yards and began to set up our defense line. But we faced in the direction of the "supply house" and its companion mounds, and not toward the slope that led to the beach. The former area was by far the more formidable.

As soon as we had our line established, Wells decided to investigate the patches of brush along our immediate front. We had given these only a quick look as we passed them. The lieutenant took with him Pfc. Donald Ruhl, our platoon malcontent. Wells had his Thompson submachine gun and Ruhl his Garand rifle, to which he'd attached his bayonet. Ruhl had much earlier discarded the helmet he hated and was wearing only a fatigue cap.

While the two were kicking around in the brush, the bypassed mound suddenly came to life. The concrete door on its right flank rolled open, and a three-inch fieldpiece, flashing orange, began to boom shells along the perimeter toward the southwest.

Wells was about to alert our platoon for an attack on the bunker when he saw that a 1st Battalion squad was already moving against it. Led by a strapping 2nd lieutenant, the men closed in swiftly, their maneuver partly screened by a scattering of bushes. Then the bunker began to spit machine gun bullets, and the advance halted as one of the leading Marines crumpled and died. But the squad soon swung around to the right, out of the machine gun's field of fire. From there a man rushed the bunker with a shape charge. He scrambled to the top of the mound, scratched away an area of sand, planted the charge, then bounded for safety. A loud blast followed, and a hole was driven down through the concrete and into the bunker. The measure wasn't strong enough to finish the occupants, but it made them hasten to close the doorway they had been firing through. Another Marine now climbed the mound and dropped a thermite grenade through the shape-charge hole.

During the foregoing action Wells and Ruhl had been working their way closer to the bunker. And now, as the thermite grenade started to generate intense heat and smoke within, they became an important part of the assault. The concrete door that faced our lines was pushed open, and a cloud of white smoke billowed out. A huddle of green sneakers appeared at its base, and the two men opened fire. Wells let go an entire 40-round Thompson clip, and Ruhl emptied his eight-shot Garand. Three Japanese stumbled out of the smoke and fell to the ground. One made a feeble attempt to rise, and Ruhl hurried forward to finish the job with his bayonet.

A moment later Wells saw a hand grenade arc toward Ruhl from a thicket several yards to the left. At the lieutenant's cry, "Look out—grenade!" Ruhl dropped flat, and the fragments lashed out harmlessly.

Wells slammed a fresh clip into his Thompson and ran toward the thicket. He was staking his life on the probability that the Japanese, since he'd done no shooting, was without a firearm. The lieutenant crouched low as he entered the brush. Dusk was setting in, and he knew his best chance of locating his quarry lay in his spotting a silhouette against the sky. But a complete search convinced him the grenadier was no longer there.

Returning to the bunker, Wells found Ruhl involved in a struggle with one of the 1st Battalion Marines who had made the assault. The man was temporarily deranged and was trying to wrest away Ruhl's bayoneted rifle, apparently wanting to use it to mutilate the fallen Japanese.

"Give it to me!" he yelled, his eyes blurred with tears. "Those son-of-a-bitches killed my buddy!"

"Take it easy! Take it easy!" Ruhl pleaded, straining to break the man's grip on his weapon. Ruhl himself had done what bayoneting he considered necessary, and all three of the Japanese were dead.

Two of the crazed Marine's friends hastened toward the scuffling pair and pulled the offender away. He calmed down as they led him back toward their unit's section of the perimeter.

The things that had happened since our platoon moved in with the 1st Battalion were significant. Our lieutenant had responded well to his first real test as a combat Marine. He had been right about the bunker and had conducted himself commendably in the action against it. We knew now that his demeanor in training, when he had quoted from Jenghiz Khan and talked dramatically about his battlefield intentions, hadn't been idle bravado. He was actually the resolute fighting man he imagined himself to be. And he was the kind of platoon leader enlisted men most respect. He wasn't content merely to issue orders; he insisted on *leading*.

Donald Ruhl, too, had proved himself aggressive. Criticized in training for his discontent and rebelliousness, he had let us know he intended to "show us" when he got into combat. And he'd made a good start. After the bunker encounter he asked to become the lieutenant's permanent runner, a job that would involve repeated exposure under fire, and Wells was glad to have him.

OUR FIRST NIGHT

Darkness was now beginning to settle over the island, and the dreaded blanket seemed almost to have an actual physical weight. Its effect on our vision increased the threat to our lives. The ground we occupied was completely unfamiliar to us, while our adversaries knew it intimately. Perhaps they had even been trained to deal with the very problem our presence had created.

The Japanese were stealthy night fighters. Skilled at infiltration tactics, they often crawled about amid their enemies and tried to kill them as they slept. It was said among the Marines that a night-creeping Japanese would sometimes feel about in a foxhole very carefully until he had touched a body, his purpose being to make sure it was warm, lest he waste a hand grenade on a corpse. Whether this particular story was true or not, it typified the audacity of the Japanese soldier. His daring sometimes went beyond the understanding of our Western minds, and we were quick to call him fanatical. We attributed his seeming fearlessness to a psychology based on a blind belief in his religion. But regardless of what one is taught he can't help but have an instinctive fear of violent death. So in the final analysis the "fanaticism" the Japanese displayed must have been prompted chiefly by courage and devotion to duty.

The Navy soon began to send up illuminating shells, and this measure would be continued until dawn. Because of the brush around us the dim light wouldn't aid our vision greatly but would cast moving shadows that gave us a start when we mistook them for skulking enemy soldiers.

We had been told to stay in our positions and keep down, since there was considerable danger of our shooting one another. A challenge-and-countersign system had been prearranged to cover the contingency of emergency move-ment. The challenger was to call out the name of an American automobile, any make, and if the challenged didn't respond immediately with the name of another make, the challenger was to shoot.

We men of Howard Snyder's squad had been assigned to the left flank of our platoon's sector. Snyder had picked a spot where two thigh-deep enemy trenches crossed each other, and we had taken cover in three segments of this junction. The fourth led toward the bunker area, and Snyder had instructed Pfc. Edward S. Kurelik, a curly headed Chicagoan, to cover its dark void with his BAR. Louie Adrian and I were in the north segment, close to the intersection. Just to our left were fire-team-leader Harold Keller and his two men, Pfc. James Robeson and Pfc. Raymond A. Strahm.

Corporal Keller was mentioned earlier as being one of our platoon's former raiders, and Robeson as being our youngest member. They made an unusual pair. One was sturdy and strong-featured, mature and calm, the very image of a fighting man, while the other was slim and animated and had a sunny, snub-nosed, whiskerless face that made him look like a typical well-favored high school student. Whereas Keller had seen extensive action, Robeson had joined the platoon straight from boot camp. The youth, however, was eager to learn and respectful of experience, and his assignment to the steady ex-raider had worked out to his advantage. Keller had advised him sensibly and patiently, and as a result he had got the most from our training program. Though Keller and the rest of us had fallen into the habit of calling Robeson "Chick" with a kind of paternal superiority, we knew that behind his boyish features there was manly resolution.

Raymond Strahm was a former paratrooper whose home was in Illinois. Several of his friends called him "Little Raymond" for a reason I never learned. He was neither little nor especially tall. Six weeks before the assault he had won the platoon's regard through a very generous act. While our regiment was aboard ship in Pearl Harbor, waiting the order to sail for its staging area, the platoon's poker players got together, and Strahm had an amazing run of luck. He broke about a dozen of us in a few hours. Soon after the game we got word that we'd be granted one final liberty in Honolulu before sailing time. But it seemed that we penniless gamblers would have to forego this pleasure. Strahm, however, promptly lent each of us ten dollars, even though he knew he'd probably never see any of the money again, since a platoon going into action has an uncertain future. We felt warmly grateful as we joined Strahm and the unit's non-gamblers in "doing the town" one more time. I myself spent part of the loan on a hula show that featured a group of chubby matrons and skinny high school girls.

(One day several years after the war I came across Strahm's home address in one of my service notebooks. Suddenly troubled about the money I owed him, I dispatched a letter in an effort to re-establish contact. The reply I received was from Strahm's wife, who informed me that my generous friend had survived the war only to die in an automobile accident soon after returning home.)

As our squad began its first fearful night on Iwo, Howard Snyder assigned us watches so at least one man would be awake and alert at all times. But there really wasn't any need for this arrangement, for most of us would think twice before we even blinked.

It soon became uncomfortably cool, the temperature dropping to about 60 degrees. As the chill penetrated our thin dungarees we began to wish we had the packs and blanket rolls we'd discarded while crossing the island. The rations in our packs, however, didn't bother us. Though I myself had eaten nothing all day except the fruit bar at noon, I hadn't the least desire for food.

Soon after dark a group of 1st Battalion Marines came walking along the perimeter from the south and passed close behind our platoon's position. These men were talking to one another in deliberately loud tones, their reason doubtless being that they didn't want to be shot by friendly troops. I wondered what sort of emergency had prompted them to make this highly dangerous move. The voices soon faded in the darkness north of us, and the group didn't return.

The naval illuminating shells enabled us to catch glimpses of Mount Suribachi through breaks in the brush. It stood about a third of a mile to our right, and was now a combination of ghostly highlights and deep shadows. Our regiment's afternoon attack on this objective had accomplished very little. The openness of the terrain, the treachery of the sand and the stubbornness of the enemy were an alliance that proved temporarily unbeatable. Originally scheduled for 3:45, the attack had been delayed by organizing difficulties until nearly 5:00 o'clock, and it had stalled soon after it was launched.

Our platoon was closer to Suribachi than it had been for most of the day, but the night's limited visibility and the clusters of brush that screened us made the volcano seem less ominous. There were two men, however, who found its presence as disturbing as ever. Corporal Robert Leader and his BAR man, Pfc. Leo Rozek, had been ordered by their squad leader, Sergeant Katie Midkiff, to occupy a barren knob that thrust itself above the bushes. Their placement was a sound tactical move, since the spot commanded a good view of the enemy areas about our platoon. But the men found themselves in a most trying situation, particularly since the knob was too solid for foxhole digging. In the fluctuating light of the illuminating shells they pressed themselves as flat as possible and imagined themselves to be the constant object of enemy observation, both from the volcano and the ground close around them. Every now and then during the long night they would make another desperate attempt to dig in, but they would be unable to do much more than scratch the knob's surface.

The detonative noises that had been so much a part of the day continued through the night but were less sustained. Volleys of small-arms fire and concentrations of shellfire, both enemy and friendly, sounded intermittently from various parts of the island. The battalion our platoon was attached to received its share of enemy shells, but our own line was overlooked.

It was believed the Japanese would launch a counterattack against the whole of our beachhead in the darkness. They were known to have a large reserve force of infantry and tanks, and this first night seemed the most likely time for the force to hit us, since we were still only shakily established on the island. But a large-scale counterattack failed to develop. At one time during the night, however, the 27th Marines, entrenched just to the north of our own regiment, discovered the enemy to be organizing along a line about five hundred yards to their front. This effort was soon broken up by artillery fire laid down by the 1st and 2nd Battalions of the 13th Marines.

Another noisy incident took place not far from our platoon. The enemy tried a barge landing on the west coast between our location and Suribachi—probably having set out from the volcano's flank—and the barge was spotted by a 1st Battalion unit that took it under fire and killed about twenty-five of its occupants.

In keeping with their reputation, the Japanese also made many individual attempts to infiltrate our lines. My squad was among those hit.

The night was dragging wretchedly. As I lay in my segment of the trench, with my rifle in my hands and my combat knife stuck into the sand within easy reach, I shivered often. The 60-degree chill seemed now to have penetrated to my bones, and the anxiety I felt increased my muscular tension. Everything, as the saying goes, is relative. The day had been bad, but its terrors dimmed when compared with those of the night. Through the daylight hours I had often thought: "What a relief it will be to see this madness end." Now, as I shuddered in the darkness, my foremost thought was this: "What a relief it will be to see daylight come." My worries were increased by the fact that the side of my trench that faced the bunker area had been blown away by a shell, and instead of having a vertical wall for protection I had only a slope. I seldom took my eyes off the slope's summit, and I expected momentarily to see a Japanese silhouette loom above it.

But when the Japanese came, during the early morning hours, he didn't come over my summit. With a hand grenade in readiness, he came creeping up the trench Ed Kurelik was covering with his BAR. I was joltingly warned of his presence by Kurelik's sharp challenge, "Studebaker!" This was immediately followed by an exclamation in Japanese and a flashing explosion in our midst. Two men were hit—Kurelik and Pfc. Phillip E. Christman, one of our Californians. The rest of us sprang up with raised rifles as our assailant darted away. Several men fired into the shadows, and Snyder threw two hand grenades that exploded brightly and peppered the brush with shrapnel. But we had no reason to believe the Japanese had been downed.

As the brief incident ended I discovered that my teeth were chattering. The sudden scare, coming as it did after I had spent seven or eight hours chilled to the bone and tensely watchful, had tested me severely. Sitting down in my trench with my back against its solid side, I clamped my jaws together firmly until the spasm passed.

Only one of our wounded men had been hit seriously. Ed Kurelik had an egg-sized hole in his thigh and a foot injury that probably involved a fracture. Phil Christman had taken fine fragments on various parts of his body. The wounds were negligible, and he would stay in the fight.

One of our platoon corpsmen, John Bradley, who was dug in some yards from our squad, made his way to the men on his hands and knees, first letting us know he was coming so we wouldn't shoot him.

Kurelik seemed to feel that the Japanese hadn't quite played fair. While Corpsman Bradley treated him he said complainingly in his pronounced Chicago accent: "I heard somebody comin' up the trench and I hollered, 'Studebaker!' And then that Jap t'rew a hand grenade!"

Kurelik seemed to be implying that if the Japanese had been a good sport he would have merely done something like holler back, "Cadillac!"

But the Chicagoan's words were also proof of his courage. Many men, after such an experience, wouldn't have expressed displeasure with the enemy's methods but only anguish at being so badly hurt.

With daylight still two or three hours away, Snyder expected more trouble and placed a second BAR man, Chick Robeson, at the danger point, telling him he was to forget about challenging and was to open fire at anything he saw moving in the trench. Most of the rest of us initiated our own nervous watch on the trench area. But the remainder of the night passed without incident.

BACK TO THE OPEN SAND

The gray arc of dawn was a beautiful sight. It signaled us the glad news that we had survived the night and would shortly be able to see again. Though the enemy would still have the powerful advantage of his fortifications, we would at least know where he was. He wouldn't be able to materialize suddenly out of a shadow at our elbow.

It was barely light before men started to stir all along our defense line. Voices that had been held to a whisper through the night became once more audible, and some of the men even reverted to their usual unrestrained profanity.

As soon as it was light enough to move safely, Sergeant Hank Hansen, our platoon guide, approached our squad to talk with Howard Snyder.

"God, what a long night!" he said with a wincing shake of his head. "What was that commotion over here?"

Snyder explained, and he and Hansen went out in front of the line to make a check, feeling that the Japanese, after all, might be lying out there dead or wounded. They found nothing, but word came up the line from the left that there was a dead Japanese officer a few yards in front of the unit next to us—and the body hadn't been noticed the preceding evening. This may or may not have been the man with whom we'd had our encounter.

I myself hadn't fired at the fleeing Japanese. On the training field I had made up my mind that I wasn't going to be "trigger happy" in combat, that I wouldn't fire unless I saw something to fire at. But perhaps a certain amount of wild shooting is a necessary part of battle. In the case of the firing my friends had done, even if it hadn't hit its intended target, it certainly must have helped to discourage other lurking Japanese from considering an attack on our section of the line.

With the coming of full daylight the reduced artillery bunker became the scene of a second incident. The 1st Battalion men who had assaulted the structure approached it out of curiosity and a wish to look for souvenirs, and they flushed another Japanese from its dark interior. As the unarmed man began to run for his life the Marine who had gone berserk at the death of his friend whipped out his combat knife and bounded into pursuit.

"Get him! Get the bastard!" his comrades cried.

As he overtook the Japanese the Marine seized him by the shoulder and drove the knife home savagely, first into his neck and then into his side. Spurting blood from the neck wound, the man dropped limply. His death was at least quick.

On every battlefield there are men who fight with a barbarian hatred. I once heard a medal-winning Marine say: "I wasn't trying to be a hero. I just hate Japs!" He doubtless thought he was being modest, but I would have preferred to believe he had been aspiring to heroism.

One of the things that caused many Marines to hate the Japanese was that they sometimes tortured their prisoners. This knowledge drove some of our men to no-quarter fighting and to the occasional use of measures that were unnecessarily brutal. These things were done, of course, in the name of retaliation. But if you were to ask a Japanese why his country's soldiers stooped to such a savagery as torture he would probably say that it was done in retaliation to similar work by Americans.

Before the battle for Iwo Jima ended, a member of our own 3rd Platoon, a good-natured and likeable youth, was, after falling wounded, stealthily seized by the Japanese and put to death by torture. A group from the platoon experienced the horror of finding his mutilated remains in a captured cave.

But I can also cite an example of brutality on the part of Iwo Jima's Marines. A Japanese who was taken prisoner at the northern end of the island was turned over to three men for delivery by jeep to their regiment's headquarters. The route was rough and rocky, and the Marines, as the jeep bounced along, "accidentally" jostled the Japanese out onto the ground. They then stopped and put him back in—only to have a similar "accident" occur a little farther along the way. They did this several times before the trip ended. One of these Marines would tell me, a month after the battle: "We got him back to headquarters alive, but he was a pretty sorry sight." If this wasn't an instance of torture, it was certainly something not very far from it.

We all have some of the savage in us. Happily not too many of us are capable of wanton brutality. Most of us, in fact, keep our brute instincts under control and do our best to steer clear of violence. But we can't help but be fascinated by it. For example: we call ourselves peace lovers but make shrines of our battlefields. And these aren't just monuments to our heroic dead. We seek them out and try to reconstruct in our imagination the awful things that happened on them. For a hundred years we Americans have been discussing Pickett's tragic charge at Gettysburg with a primitive enjoyment.

But perhaps our interest in violence isn't really something to be deplored. Perhaps our survival as a nation depends on our not becoming too civilized. It wasn't intellectual pacifism that kept us free since 1776. It was the willingness of our people to turn to violent measures when the need arose.

Poncho being used as a stretcher.

Photo by Lou Lowery

Today there are still would-be world conquerors. And such men have always been notoriously deaf to pacifistic pleas. World peace is a noble goal, but the bitter truth is that not even the wisest among us have yet figured out how we can stay free without sometimes taking up arms.

In the Atomic Age, of course, this truth is particularly frightening. But even so, none of us should be too strongly pacifistic. After all, we're supposed to be a people who love liberty above life.

The 3rd Platoon had new orders to follow this second morning on Iwo Jima. We were to start working our way back across the island toward our own battalion's zone on the left of the lines facing Mount Suribachi. By late afternoon we would be needed at the unit's front. The 1st Battalion would spend the day reorganizing and completing its job of mopping up the scrub-wood, while the 3rd Battalion would continue in its position on the right of the Suribachi attack.

Before our platoon moved out, Corpsman Bradley re-dressed Ed Kurelik's thigh and foot wounds. Then four of the Chicagoan's friends spread a poncho on the ground and had him maneuver himself to its center. When each of the men wrapped a corner securely about a fist and lifted, Kurelik found himself in a passable litter. He would be left with the first group of wounded we met.

Sunlight was filtering through the brush now, and we welcomed its warmth. After making our way along the night defense line toward Suribachi for fifty or sixty yards, we entered an antitank ditch that led in the direction of the east coast. We stayed in this excavation, which was occupied also by a 1st Battalion platoon, for an hour or more.

There was a poncho-covered dead Marine lying near the spot where we members of Howard Snyder's squad were seated. We learned from the man's friends that he had suffered a lonely and lingering death. The evening before, while he was walking from his company's headquarters to the place where his squad was dug in, he took a machine gun burst in the back. He cried out as he fell, and his friends shouted to him an anxious query as to what had happened. But they got no reply. With darkness setting in and movement becoming extra-dangerous, they decided to stay in their holes. They figured that the man, since he hadn't answered, was probably beyond their help anyway. But when morning came and they were able to go to him they found him still alive—though only barely. He had lain all night, completely incapacitated, where he fell. And he died soon after feebly pointing out the bunker from which he'd been shot. The man's friends were now digging a shallow temporary grave for him, and an assault squad was preparing to reduce the bunker.

Since it stood near the rim of our ditch, we could watch the demolitions men work. No opposition developed as they readied their deadly charges. The mound remained tightly sealed. It was obvious that the men inside, who had dared to fire under cover of dusk, had been trying to remain inconspicuous since the coming of daylight. Surrounded by Marines, they knew that to call attention to themselves would only hasten their extermination. They were probably hoping we would figure their fortification to be deserted and would move on without blowing it. It appeared that at least some of our Iwo enemies, in spite of the reputation the Japanese had for being fanatical fighters, were, after all, only fear-prone, life-loving men like ourselves. But we could feel no compassion for the bunker's occupants. It was a distinct relief to see this threat to our security removed. The demolitions men first used a charge to blow open a firing aperture and then quickly thrust another charge inside. As the second blast rocked the mound we felt certain its whole crew had been destroyed.

Our attention was next drawn to Mount Suribachi, which had now become the object of attack. Groups of Marine and Navy aircraft, flying low, began to roar in from the west and hit the volcano's base and slopes with rockets, bombs and machine gun bullets. Their napalm bombs erupted into great searing sheets of flame. From ships lying close to shore on both flanks came shells and more rockets. And artillery pieces on the island added their own heavy projectiles to the effort. The jumble of explosions and the thunder of the planes were a deafening combination, and the air about us and the earth beneath us seemed alive with vibration. The attack, in addition to being destructive, had a definite morale value. We infantrymen, who had to face the enemy with relatively puny weapons, were dramatically reminded that we had some powerful assistance.

Soon after the action started I noticed that a 1st Battalion Marine who was sitting across the antitank ditch from me had been hit in the mouth by a piece of shrapnel, and I realized the Japanese were doing some shelling of their own. Fortunately most of the shells were landing not in our ditch but along its rim. Our position was also covered by rifle fire. This discovery was made by a group who climbed the wall of the ditch to get a better view of the Suribachi attack. I saw them make a quick retraction down the slope after being narrowly missed by a spattering of bullets.

When we at last began to head back across the island, we moved through the scrubwood along a route that was similar to the one we had used while going in the opposite direction the day before. And we once more took full advantage of the cover afforded by the network of antitank ditches and trenches. The bunkers and pillboxes we saw gave us moments of uneasiness, though most appeared to have been assaulted. We passed several 1st Battalion aid stations. Some of the wounded had been waiting evacuation since the day before.

We didn't have to expose ourselves often, since the trenches and ditches were pretty well interconnected. But this arrangement at one time came close to working against us. While our assault squad was leading the way from a ditch into a narrow connecting trench, a Marine in the ditch our men were heading for shouted, "Watch yourselves! There's a machine gun trained down that trench!"

This prompted the assault squad to turn and start running back toward the ditch that held the rest of us. Lieutenant Wells was just starting to enter the trench, and he was knocked down and run over.

"Dammit!" he said as he struggled to his feet. "What happened?"

After the men explained, the lieutenant sent a rifleman up on each flank of the trench to look for the Japanese gun. They saw nothing, so Wells decided to have us run through, one at a time. He himself led the way. This was a nerve-racking dash, but we all made it without drawing fire.

In the new ditch we came upon a badly wounded and gruesomely blood-spattered Marine. He had been treated by a corpsman but was now sitting alone halfway up one of the excavation's sloping sides. His eyes were glassy with shock. He had apparently been the victim of machine gun fire, for even now there were bullets raking the sandy rim above his head.

As soon as our lieutenant's runner, Donald Ruhl, spotted the man he determined to take him to an aid station. Wells was opposed to this, since he wanted to keep his platoon intact. All too often when a man left a unit on such an errand he failed to return. But Ruhl, enlisting the help of a friend, hurried to the wounded man's side. Staying below the machine gun fire, the pair eased the man down the bank. Then, each of them grasping a blood-smeared arm and hooking it about the back of his neck, they began to carry-walk the dazed figure toward the east coast. Ruhl hollered over his shoulder to Wells that they'd be back shortly. The runner himself kept his promise, but he earned our lieutenant's anger by losing his helper somewhere along the way.

While we were lingering in another ditch an extraordinary thing happened where Howard Snyder and I were located. We were startled to hear a Japanese light machine gun open fire in the brush not more than fifteen or twenty yards from the rim above our heads.

Snyder quickly clambered up the slope and peered in the direction of the sound.

"See anything?" I asked.

He kept his voice low as he answered, "The brush is too thick."

At that moment a lone 1st Battalion Marine who was walking through the ditch approached our position. He was bare-headed and without a jacket, and he had his shirt sleeves rolled up. His bearing was jaunty, and his rifle swung lightly in his right hand. Hearing the *pup-pup-pup* of the Japanese gun he stopped and said, "That sounds like a Nambu."

"It is," Snyder told him. "But I can't spot it."

"I'll find it," the stranger said simply, and he climbed the slope and disappeared into the bushes along its summit.

For a few minutes the machine gun kept up its regular *pup-pup-pupping*. Then it was interrupted by several shots from a Garand rifle. These were immediately followed by a sustained burst from the Nambu. Then the Garand crashed three more times. With that the brush was still.

Shortly afterward the stranger was sliding back down the slope of our ditch. In addition to the rifle in his right hand he was now carrying, on his left shoulder, a Japanese light machine gun. Blood was trickling from a bullet hole in the outside of his right biceps, but he was grinning.

"I hope this thing cost those bastards a lot of money," he said.

Then before we could question him about his feat he continued along the ditch with the same jaunty air that had marked his arrival.

We had witnessed a phenomenon: an example of valor in the romantic tradition. Unfortunately this lighthearted hero wouldn't receive a medal for his achievement. He hadn't been seen by anyone who knew him and could make the recommendation.

Our platoon reached the eastern fringe of the scrubwood, at a point about two hundred yards behind the lines facing Suribachi, shortly before noon. We were now in the last antitank ditch available to us, and our lieutenant crawled up its terminal slope and scanned the barren sand for a possible sheltered spot where we could begin our wait, as a 2nd Battalion reserve unit, for our call to the front.

With Wells taking the lead, our column's foremost men soon began to leave the ditch in trotting groups. When the lieutenant called a temporary halt to the advance a few moments later I was just climbing out of the ditch, and I found myself in a spot where I still had good cover but could observe much of the Suribachi action.

The volcano was still being pounded steadily by land, sea and air, and was giving off many trailings of smoke. Most of our frontline riflemen, machine gunners and mortar-men were hidden in the sand, but our tanks were lumbering about openly. They hadn't been able to come forward until 11:00 o'clock because of refueling and rearming difficulties but were now in effective operation. The 37-millimeter guns and the 75-millimeter halftracks of our regimental weapons company had been moved close to the front so they might better fire on the squat fortifications that semicircled Suribachi's base.

But the puffs of sand and smoke that were rising among our own positions indicated that the Japanese were managing to fight back vigorously. Our front lines, in fact, had been able to advance only sixty or seventy yards all morning.

As my eyes flicked back to the volcano they were drawn to one of its caves. Standing boldly in the entrance, one on either side of an artillery piece, were two Japanese. They were so far from my position as to be barely distinguishable, but a careful look assured me they were indeed there. Both were stripped to the waist, and one had a white bandage about his head. It was the bandage,

I believe, that first caught my attention. Defiantly manning their gun in the face of the overwhelming odds we presented, the pair made a heroic picture. (Naturally I wasn't strongly aware of this at the time, but today I can consider the scene objectively.) Spread over the ocean to their right and left were scores of our ships; in the air above them were several groups of snarling planes; and on the field before them were thousands of Marines and an ominous deployment of heavy weapons. Their fortress was still fairly secure, but they must have known that its days were numbered and that they must soon die. One of them had apparently already been wounded. These men were the enemy, but they were no less heroes than the Americans who fought to the death defending the Alamo.

Wells presently signaled the resumption of our trotting move across the sand, and within a few minutes our entire column was clear of the scrubwood. As we passed a large pile of K-rations that had been brought inland by one of our tracked supply craft, each of us stopped briefly to snatch up two or three boxes.

We were soon settled in a long shallow excavation that ran east and west and had sand heaped high all along its southern rim. The ditch had been dug by the Japanese for a purpose unknown to us, but we discovered its sandbank to be excellent protection from the volcano's fire.

Most of us shortly started to tear open our K-rations to do the first real eating we had done for thirty hours. In spite of our apprehensions we had finally begun to feel hunger pangs. Nature had begun to let us know that we needed refueling in order to carry on.

Machine gun fire from Suribachi several times swept the top of our parapet while we ate, the bullets plucking shrilly at the sand and scattering grains of it over us. Since we were in no danger from this fire we paid it little attention.

I found myself feeling safer here than I had felt at any time since we landed. When I finished eating I lay back against the sandbank, closed my eyes and turned my face up to the warm sun. Soon some of the tension left my muscles and I was drowsing. The island's noises had dimmed in my ears until they were only vaguely disturbing.

I enjoyed this respite for all of ten minutes. Then Howard Snyder nudged me and said, "Wheeler, let's you and I go hunt our packs."

This was a most unwelcome proposal. But I still hadn't given up trying to appear as courageous as my friend, so I answered, "Sounds like a good idea."

Our search carried us over an area of sand that stretched about two hundreds yards to the rear of the parapet. There was no cover, and we offered fine targets for both shellfire and bullets. Even the scrubwood on our flank was still a grave threat. Our danger was increased by the fact that we were the only ones in the vicinity who were on our feet, and were therefore extra-conspicuous.

We came upon several groups of Marines who were huddled in foxholes. These men looked up at us, owl-eyed, as we passed. I envied them their concealment, and I silently cursed myself for the pride that made me do things I didn't really have the guts for. I would have much preferred being chilly at night to risking my life for covering.

After a ten-minute hunt we found our packs. In the same area I found a new fully-loaded .45 caliber pistol. I considered this a real treasure, since there are times in close-quarters combat when the pistol can prove a readier weapon than the rifle.

On our return trip we passed a Marine who was lying immobile on the sand. He had no visible wound but looked as though he had just lain down on his side and gone to sleep. He must have come ashore only a short time before with a reserve unit, for he was clean and neat and had all his gear arranged on his person according to regulations.

When we were perhaps fifty feet past the body Snyder said, "I guess we should have stopped and made sure that fellow was dead."

War dogs were invaluable aids in detecting skulking enemy soldiers. This dog is standing guard—infallibly— while his master naps.

Marine Corps Photo

"He was dead," I answered with assurance. "His lips were blue."

But even as I spoke I wondered whether this was a definite indication of death. At the old swimming hole of my childhood I had seen a lot of blue-lipped boys who were very much alive. But Snyder didn't question my statement, and we kept going.

Our returning with our packs made us the envy of our squad, and several of the men decided to go look for their own. But these searchers, led by Raymond Strahm, had traveled only about twenty-five yards when they drew machine gun fire. It came from the left, from the scrubwood. The men turned and broke for the parapet, and Snyder and I watched bullets kick up sand behind them as they ran. They all made it back, landing in the ditch with such force that some of us had to dodge to keep from being trampled.

Breathing hard after the experience, Strahm exclaimed to Snyder and me, "You lucky son-of-a-guns!"

Further attempts at pack-retrieving were, for the time being, abandoned.

Snyder and I now set about reorganizing our packs and discarding everything we felt was nonessential. I saved only my poncho, a spare jacket, a couple of changes of underwear and socks, a few toilet articles, writing paper and envelopes, and the special stock of canned foods I had bought in Honolulu—such delicacies as boned turkey, boned chicken and maraschino cherries.

(One of the things I discarded that afternoon was a small book entitled *A Brief American Literature*. I had bought this in a secondhand bookstore in California a year before and had become quite fond of it, even though it was thirty-five years old. I had read it several times and had filled its flyleaves with notes regarding its contents, and when its binding had begun to go I repaired it with adhesive tape. When I laid the book aside on Iwo Jima I naturally assumed I would never see it again. But my name, too, was written on one of its flyleaves. And two years after the war I got a letter from a Marine Corps salvage unit to the effect that some of my belongings had turned up. Did I want them? I returned the required form, and a few weeks later I received a small carton. And it contained only one item, my *Brief American Literature*. There were grains of Iwo's sand among its pages. Today the tired little volume, bearing a 1909 copyright date, still occupies a revered place on one of my bookshelves.)

We waited behind our parapet for several hours. No one paid much attention to the Suribachi action except for those times when it suddenly intensified. Then a few of us would climb the parapet and look over it and try to figure out what was going on.

Most of us had reached a point where we didn't think too often about the problems ahead. There was usually enough anxiety connected with the moment at hand. When the order came we would start toward the volcano; then if the situation was bad we'd worry about it. In the meantime we would merely sit in the sun against our sandbank, feeling fairly safe from small-arms fire and hoping that no shells would land among us.

WE FACE THE VOLCANO

It was about 4:00 o'clock when we got the order to head for the front. We were to relieve our company's 1st Platoon, whose leaders were 1st Lieutenant George E. Stoddard and Platoon Sergeant Paul P. Paljavcsick. The unit had been on the line for some hours and had lost a number of men, Lieutenant Stoddard himself having been wounded.

Our battalion had made some gains during the afternoon, and the front was now about three hundred yards ahead of us. Since the trip would take us over wholly open ground and there would be no place for us to rendezvous before our deployment, Lieutenant Wells decided to make a personal reconnaissance of the line before having us come up. Platoon Sergeant Thomas, after waiting about fifteen minutes, was to start sending us up in small groups to be placed on the line as we arrived. Wells felt that this procedure would not only minimize the confusion of the deployment but would keep our unit less conspicuous than if we moved up in force.

The lieutenant covered about two-thirds of the distance to the front without much trouble. Then a machine gun on Suribachi opened up on him. As bullets began to cut into the sand beside him he veered away and jumped into a broad but shallow crater. Lying against one of its sides was a Marine with bloody chest wounds that appeared to be mortal. Still conscious, he was breathing heavily through his mouth.

It would seem a man in such a state would have thoughts only for himself. But this man yelled: "Get out of here! They've got this hole covered!"

As Wells sprang from the crater he dropped the poncho that had been folded into the rear of his belt, and he glanced back to see it being chewed up by Japanese bullets. This spurred him to race for a nearby mound of sand, which he dived behind.

In the meantime Ernest Thomas had been ordered by a higher officer to take our entire platoon to the front immediately. And in spite of our lieutenant's instructions the sergeant had to do as he was told.

We left our parapet by filing around its left flank, and as soon as we were in the open we felt naked and vulnerable. During our wait we had at times almost forgotten Mount Suribachi, but suddenly there it was again, smoking under our regiment's attack but looking bigger and more menacing than ever.

Within a few minutes we were engulfed by the action, and its noise and fury increased as we advanced. The sand around us held booming howitzers, tanks, halftracks and 37-millimeter guns. Also firing earnestly, though less visibly, were many of the mortars and machine guns of our weapons platoons. Because of the field's activity our move wasn't noticeable enough to invite a concentration of enemy fire, but we were conscious of some close shellbursts and the sporadic whine of bullets.

Wells was still pinned down behind the sand pile as we drew near him, and the unexpected sight of us made him furious. He said afterward that we came "not as I ordered but like a band of Comanches, with Thomas in the lead. I was never so mad in my life." He shouted and signaled for us to take cover and watched us scatter "like a bunch of goddamned quail."

Wanting to tell him what had happened, Thomas continued toward him. He ran first for the hole that held the dying Marine and the riddled poncho, and he didn't immediately comprehend the lieutenant's urgent warning that he avoid it. But at the last moment he altered his course and headed for the mound where Wells lay, shortly dropping beside him on the sand.

By this time one of our own machine gunners had spotted the source of the lieutenant's plight, and after a brief duel the Japanese gun fell silent.

Two tanks, having been ordered to cover the last hundred yards of our advance, now lumbered toward us from the direction of the front. We regarded their arrival with mixed feelings. Their atmosphere of power was comforting, but we knew they might at any second draw fire from the enemy's heaviest weapons.

We hadn't dispersed as widely as Wells feared, and he and Thomas were soon able to get us into two irregular columns behind the tanks. They began to grind forward clumsily, rising and falling on the uneven sand and throwing up sprays of it with their creaking tracks. As we slogged along in their wake they fired their 75-millimeter guns, trying to make the Japanese ahead keep under cover and keep their resistance at a minimum. After each blast a large shell casing was ejected out onto the sand. One of these brushed the hand of Pfc. Graydon W. "Grady" Dyce, a lean fairskinned South Dakotan, and stung him with its heat.

Mount Suribachi's gray dome was now rising above us in staggering proportions. The sun had slipped behind it and we were moving in its shadow, and this magnified its forbidding aspect.

Some of us began to notice Japanese activity in the brush that covered the volcano's approaches. Now and then a man would stop briefly and let go a few ill-aimed shots. Several men at this time made the alarming discovery that their weapons were sand-jammed.

As we reached the first of the front-line troops I passed a rifleman who was lying on his stomach in a shallow hole and was sighting toward the brush.

"How's it going up here?" I shouted to him.

His answering shout was hardly reassuring: "We're getting shot to hell!"

When our advance at last halted and we took cover we were part of a line that was a scant two hundred yards from Suribachi's first defenses. But even at this distance there wasn't much discernible. We saw the same battered block-house walls we had seen from a distance and a few smaller concrete structures whose sand had been blown away, but that was about all. The majority of the caves were as obscure as the bunkers, pillboxes and trenches. Even those entrances on the volcano's steep slopes were most of them hidden by clefts and shadows. Judged by appearances Mount Suribachi was no more than an enormous green-skirted mound of rock and dirt. But we knew we were facing one of the most ingenious fortresses ever conceived.

For some unknown reason the Japanese gave us little trouble as we deployed. This surprised us, since we had assumed that once we were in this close it would be almost impossible for us to move without drawing fire.

The area held a generous scattering of bomb craters and shell holes, and we took to them in two- and three-man groups. We of Howard Snyder's squad, ordered into platoon reserve, settled about twenty-five yards behind the forward line. Wells probably picked us for the reserve spot because we had been grenaded the night before and had spent the hours even less restfully than his other squads.

While the lieutenant was setting up his command post he chanced to look toward the edge of Suribachi's brush and see the tops of several enemy heads in a hole he believed to be a mortar pit. He had discovered a job for a tank, but the two that had covered our approach had already withdrawn. There was one firing from a position in front of the platoon on our right, however, and he decided to run over to it.

He took with him Corporal Robert M. Lane, the leader of our 2nd squad. Lane, a red-haired Arkansan, was quiet and reserved, not easy to know; but he was a former raider, which was enough to assure us of his battlefield competence.

When the pair reached the tank they found two dead Marines lying beside it. Its telephone was on the sand with a mangled wire. The men had been shot down while informing the crew of a target, and the phone they dropped had been backed over.

Wells was carrying his Thompson, and he used its butt to pound on the side of the tank to get its crew's attention. Then he pointed toward the enemy emplacement, and the tank's gunner soon spotted the heads. After firing several rounds he made a direct hit, and Wells and Lane saw one of the Japanese fly into the air. They could only guess at the fate of the others.

Lane took the lead on the return run, the lieutenant following closely. Suddenly a heavy shell exploded right behind Wells. Its concussion threw him astride Lane's back, and both men sprawled to the sand. They were remarkably lucky. The shell had buried itself so deeply before bursting that Wells received only a few sandblast scratches and Lane wasn't touched. Relieved to find themselves unhurt, they rose and resumed running, and

Corporal Robert M. Lane in 1944, when he became leader of the 3rd Platoon's 2nd Squad.

Studio Photo

they were about recovered from the experience by the time they got back to the platoon.

With darkness now only an hour or two away, the attack on the volcano diminished. The last of our tanks were withdrawing to their night stations, and our planes were returning to their carriers. We infantrymen, left largely to our own resources, went on the defensive. Our assault would not be renewed until morning.

Howard Snyder, Louie Adrian and I had taken cover together. In keeping with his indifference to danger Snyder had picked us a *shallow* crater, even though there were deep ones nearby. When we sat up, our heads and shoulders were above its rim. This gave us a fine view of Mount Suribachi, but it also gave the volcano a pretty good view of us. And since there were said to be about two thousand Japanese manning its defenses I found myself feeling completely outstared.

The first thing we did after getting settled was clean our rifles. I also field-stripped the .45 caliber pistol I had found. After dusting it and putting it back together I slipped it into one of the socks from my pack, leaving only its handle exposed. Having this hard-hitting weapon thrust into my belt gave me a good feeling. I had always liked handguns, and I valued the .45 above my rifle.

During these moments Louie Adrian looked toward the volcano and saw a Japanese dart from a cleft at its base and enter a clump of brush. The Indian readied his BAR and watched the spot for a time, but the man didn't reappear.

Shortly afterward Chick Robeson and Phil Christman approached our crater, and Robeson said, "Wells wants four men from our squad to go back for barbed wire."

Snyder asked Adrian and me to join the pair for this task. We had to go back about a hundred yards to Easy Company headquarters, and we made the trip on the run. With the sand yielding under our feet running wasn't easy, but we weren't encumbered with gear. We carried only our weapons, having left even our cartridge belts behind. I myself carried only my trusty pistol.

At headquarters, which had been set up in the entrance section of a large isolated bunker, we found Captain Dave Severance, Lieutenant Harold Schrier, 1st Sergeant John A. Daskalakis and Gunnery Sergeant Philip F. Strout making their own preparations for the night. We saw also Pfc. Leonard J. Mooney, of Hackettstown, New Jersey, who had been with the 3rd Platoon through most of its training but was now handling the captain's communications equipment.

We were given two coils of wire. They weren't heavy, and since there were two of us for each we were able to run for most of the trip back. We took the wire to the very front, to the shell hole where Wells had his command post. Then we returned, once more on the run, to the welcome semi-security of our own craters. In spite of the fact that we had been within easy range of enemy guns for the whole of our mission, we had drawn no fire.

About fifteen minutes later the lieutenant called for another group from our squad to help stretch the wire and set up trip flares out in front of the line. I wasn't assigned to this detail but Adrian, Robeson and Christman were. They were joined by Ernest Thomas, Bob Lane, Clarence Hipp, Pfc. William J. McNulty and Wells himself. These men had to expose themselves starkly. They worked fast, talking as little as possible and in subdued tones, expecting momentarily to feel the impact of enemy bullets. None came, however, and they were soon finished and making a safe return to their craters.

Battlefield situations like this defy understanding. We men of the wire details must have been observed by many of the enemy, and we would have made easy targets. But not a weapon was raised against us.

Our platoon's position began to seem considerably less perilous than I had believed it would be. I wondered whether the Japanese were saving their ammunition for the close-quarters attack they knew we would launch in the morning.

Marine radio operator.

Marine Corps Photo

Gaining a little spirit from this line of thinking I took a can of boned turkey from my pack, opened it with my combat knife and began to eat. When I bought this delicacy in Honolulu I had pictured myself eating it during a lull in the fighting, even as I was now doing. But I had imagined myself enjoying it. As it turned out, I might as well have been downing my least-liked type of K-ration, for the turkey, with the volcano watching me, was tasteless. It was merely an item of nourishment, something I knew my body needed to maintain its strength for the ordeals ahead.

Snyder and the Indian had their own rations, and they too began to eat. But we were shortly interrupted by the nearby crash of a mortar shell. It seemed as though the enemy had deliberately waited until this moment to open fire. The burst marked the beginning of an intensive shelling, the worst we had yet undergone. Up and down our lines the explosions walked, spewing steel and sand in all directions. Snyder, Adrian and I thrust aside our food and pressed ourselves as low as we could in our shallow crater.

The dread this shellfire caused our platoon was accompanied by a feeling of helplessness. There was nothing we could do but cower in our holes and take it. In the first place, the pits it was coming from were well concealed. And even if we had been able to pinpoint them we couldn't have done anything against them with our rifles.

When one of the shells burst very close to our own crater, Snyder exclaimed, "Damn! If I knew where they were firing from we'd sure go after them!"

And for the first time since we'd landed I myself felt a stirring of aggressiveness. Snyder's words should have struck me as fantastic. To go after the mortarmen we would have had to press across two hundred yards of open sand into the volcano's belt of defenses. But our plight seemed so critical that I had begun to feel, as Snyder must have felt, that we might as well get hit while trying to do something as while cringing in a hole waiting for our luck to run out.

Up in our platoon's forward line Hank Hansen and Robert Leader shared a crater. Hansen had the audacity to stick his head up and watch the shelling, and he noticed that it was being done by pattern. It would start on the left of our sector and jump a few yards along our lines with each explosion. When it reached our right flank it would start working its way back. Hansen once watched it move along his own line and approach his own position. Suddenly he pulled his head down and shouted to Leader, "Duck! The next one's coming close!" And it did—but it failed to explode. All the pair heard was the thump of a dud somewhere near them.

Several of the men around our lieutenant's command post tried to joke to cover their nervousness. After a close burst one hollered, "Knock, knock. Who's there?" Another asked Wells what he thought his girl friend was doing at that moment. "I don't rightly know," the lieutenant said. "But by God she'd better be thinking of me!"

During the pounding my two companions and I were missed three times by only a few feet. The third shell exploded on the rim of our crater and showered us with sand.

But there's a military saying that "no situation, however hot, stays hot very long." And about the time we decided we could take no more, the shelling let up.

Wells was afraid the platoon had been torn apart, but the good luck we'd been enjoying was still holding. Only one man had been hit. Private Ogle T. Lemon had taken a blast of fine fragments on the chest. Lemon, a genial, mild-mannered Texan, was one of our older members and was well established as a family man. He was the father of two children.

In view of our light damage, it might seem that I have exaggerated this shelling. But men who have good cover and are well dispersed are not really easy targets for shellfire. The forty-three members of our platoon occupied about fifteen shell holes spread over an area of about 1,500 square yards. Even though our craters were quite broad, averaging perhaps twelve square yards at the rim, they took up only about 180 square yards in aggregate. By far the greater portion of our area was open sand.

Of course, this sort of reasoning isn't likely to be done by men being shelled. With the noise deafening and the ground trembling beneath them, all they can think about is that shells do sometimes land in holes where men are huddled. On Iwo, in fact, this was a fairly common occurrence. But for every shell that found a target there were many that exploded without effect.

After the shelling, we returned uneasily to our preparations for the night. Snyder, Adrian and I first finished eating. My turkey was now not only tasteless but almost impossible to swallow. I had to resort to washing it down with water as I had done with the fruit bar the day before.

About a half hour before dark a group of our company's machine gunners, walking in a well-spaced double file and conversing in surprisingly nonchalant tones, approached the front on our left. They had been assigned to the company's 2nd Platoon, whose leader was 2nd Lieutenant Edward S. Pennell, and they were being led up by Pennell's platoon sergeant, Joseph McGarvey.

McGarvey was from Philadelphia; he knew that I too was from eastern Pennsylvania, and as he and the group passed about twenty-five yards from me he called cheerfully, "Hiya, Wheeler! How do you think the Phillies will make out this year?"

The question came unexpectedly, and all I could think of hollering back was an insipid, "Good, I hope!"

McGarvey's greeting was obvious bravado, but this sort of thing was excellent for morale. As long as men could pretend to be light-hearted the situation didn't seem entirely hopeless.

Both leaders of the 2nd Platoon would later perform feats of valor that would earn them decorations. Lieutenant Pennell would receive the Navy Cross and Sergeant McGarvey the Silver Star.

One man who didn't seem at all bothered by the nearness of Suribachi that evening was Chuck Lindberg, the sturdy ex-raider who led our assault squad and handled one of its flame throwers. He was a dedicated souvenir hunter, and as soon as he got his squad settled he went over to the platoon's right flank to investigate the diggings around an abandoned Japanese gun pit. When he returned, he came to the hole I was in to show me one of the objects he had found, a neatly catalogued Japanese stamp collection. He seated himself on the crater's rim, and I reluctantly drew myself up beside him. Then he calmly paged through the album for my benefit. I pretended interest but was much too conscious of our danger to really see the stamps. My chief thought about the paging was that it wasn't being done nearly fast enough. Lindberg seemed to give no consideration to the fact that we might be picked off at any second. When he finally left I slid back into the crater with a feeling of relief. It seemed incredible to me that anyone could be thinking about souvenirs at a time like this.

I admired our platoon's former raiders very much. They were uncommonly good men. But I had begun to wonder how they had managed to survive several bloody battles. I had about decided that I wouldn't survive this one if I kept trying to do as they did.

But now the act I had been maintaining paid off in the form of a commendation from my friend Snyder. He told me he liked my steadiness under fire and was glad to have me with him. This meant a lot to me, though honesty almost made me confess that most of those times when he thought me courageously steady I was probably closer to being petrified.

At dusk Ernest Thomas came to our crater to consult for a few minutes with Snyder. One of the first things he said was, "Did you hear about Sergeant Plumer? He was killed this afternoon. Imagine—a nice fellow like Plumer!" Thomas, who was seeing his first combat, was clearly having trouble accepting the fact that a man he liked had been killed. His attitude seemed odd. Sergeant Plumer, a member of another platoon of Easy Company, was indeed a nice fellow. But there seemed little doubt that a lot of nice fellows were going to be killed before the fight ended. As it would turn out, Fate had arranged for the list of dead to include likeable Ernest Thomas himself.

That evening, for the first time since coming ashore, I felt the need to move my bowels. Just before dark I crept out of the crater, scooped a hole in the sand and relieved myself. During our training days I had heard many joking remarks about a Marine's needing plenty of extra underwear on the battlefield. Fear was supposed to make for bowel looseness. I myself hadn't been affected this way. But perhaps there were men who had. One member of our platoon, as soon as we hit the beach, had taken his combat knife and put a slit in the seat of his trousers and his "skivvies." He explained that he did this so he would not only be completely ready for emergency bowel movements but could have them without exposing the white of his buttocks to enemy snipers.

With the coming of darkness the Navy once more began to send illuminating shells over the island. They didn't help us much to distinguish Japanese activity on the volcano, since their unsteadiness kept its rugged surface a mass of motion; but they enabled us to get a fairly constant view of the open stretch between our lines and the first defenses. The men in the forward squads spent much of the night anxiously scanning the strip of sand that held their barbed wire and trip flares. Since the Japanese hadn't counterattacked in force the first night, it was believed they might on the second.

Soon after dark our lieutenant got a call on his telephone from company headquarters. Captain Severance had some heavy demolitions, some flares and two cans of water for our platoon. Wells decided to go back for the stuff himself, taking Clarence Hipp with him. The pair made their way by following the telephone line, and they talked loudly the whole trip to keep from being shot by Marines with nervous trigger fingers.

Wells found himself strangely irritated by the sight of the company command post. "I guess it was jealousy," he said later, "but inside me I hated every man in that secure place."

Actually, the captain and his staff weren't as safe as they seemed. At this point, there still wasn't a safe place on the whole island.

To keep from becoming accustomed to being away from the front, Wells and Hipp quickly loaded up and left. Wells carried the two heavy water cans, and Hipp the demolitions and flares. Again following the phone line and talking loudly, they reached their starting point without incident.

The squad that Donald Ruhl, the lieutenant's runner, had joined for the night was located near the abandoned gun emplacement and diggings where Chuck Lindberg had found the stamp album. Ruhl boldly explored this area in the dark, knowing full well that some of the enemy might still be lurking in it. He discovered a pitch-black tunnel leading off from the gun pit, and he had the incredible nerve to push into it and investigate its entire length with the aid of lighted matches. He found a lot of enemy gear, including a number of woolen blankets. These he carried across the shadowy sand to Wells and the men around him for use in the cool night, an act that was much appreciated. Ruhl seemed intent on making us eat the critical words we had spoken about his independence and hard-headedness in training.

The shells sent against the volcano by the Navy, the 13th Marines and our company mortar units during the night burst vividly among its restless shadows, and many of the explosions gave rise to billowy white mushrooms.

Suribachi was also the background for another type of light. The Japanese sent forth white and amber pyrotechnic signals that called for shellfire from the north of the island. One variety of missile these flares brought down on us was a particularly frightful thing. It approached with a weird screeching noise and it burst with a tremendous concussion. We learned later that it was a monstrous rocket-powered bomb that was loaded with odds and ends of scrap metal.

With a lucky shell, the enemy eventually scored a direct hit on one of the ammunition dumps on the beach to our left-rear. This set off a spectacular fireworks display. The series of explosions and red flashes continued for perhaps an hour, sometimes diminishing for a few minutes but then bursting forth with renewed brilliance. During this time the volcano and the reaches of sand around us took on a fluctuating red glow. The effect was an eerie one. It was as though our evil little island had suddenly been transported to hell.

Suribachi's defenders made one attempt to counterattack. They began to mass and organize on a plateau that lay along the volcano's left flank. But the *Henry A. Wiley,* a destroyer that was covering this area, spotted the activity and quickly closed in to two hundred yards to contest it. Switching on a powerful searchlight, the vessel opened up with all of its bearing guns. We watched with fascination while a thunder-and-lightning concentration of shellbursts and ricocheting 20-millimeter tracers raked the plateau for fifteen minutes. The organizing Japanese were decimated, and the plan to counterattack was abandoned.

There was one infiltration attempt made in our platoon's sector. The lone Japanese tried to come through on our right flank. He was dispatched by rifle fire.

Snyder, Adrian and I took turns at watches through the night. We used my pistol as our watch weapon. This night, in spite of its perils, its noises and its unearthly illuminations, was a better one for the three of us than the first had been. This time we knew we were surrounded by Marines, and we weren't cold. Snyder and I had our ponchos, and Adrian was wearing the extra jacket I had been carrying in my pack. He also had a cellophane cape from a gas mask pouch, and he used this to cover his legs. All three of us managed to get snatches of sleep. Our naps, at best, were troubled ones; but they helped in a small way to strengthen our muscles and our minds for the awful test we now had to face.

THE CHARGE

Our second dawn on Iwo Jima wasn't as welcome a sight as the first had been. As Mount Suribachi's hazy dome began to outline itself against the sky we became fully aware of what we were up against. We were now going to have to make a frontal assault, across a 200-yard open stretch, into the volcano's maze of defenses. And there wasn't much doubt that we'd be fiercely resisted. The time had come when the Japanese had to repel us or die.

The day broke quietly enough. There was at first little firing from either side, a situation that contrasted sharply with the happenings of the night. But the stillness wasn't one that made for easy breathing, for a sinister tension hung over the sand. This was the calm before the storm. It was a time of last-minute prayers and melancholy thoughts. We'd reached a point where it seemed unlikely we'd ever again see the homes that lay thousands of miles across the restless water to our left. Though we'd all joined the Marines expecting tough assignments, the thing we were about to do seemed suicidal.

As soon as it was light enough to see, our lieutenant crawled out of his crater and squatted in front of it to study the enemy's lines. Visibility soon began to improve, and he suddenly spotted a squatting Japanese who appeared to be making a study of *our* lines. Wells had left his Thompson in his crater, so he pointed out the man to the squad nearest him. But the Japanese seemed to realize what was happening. He stood up, placed his hands boldly on his hips for a moment, then strode back into the brush before our men could shoot.

The stillness in our zone was soon broken by the crackle of rifle fire along our right front. One of our squads had spotted a bustling of enemy activity in a network of shallow trenches that lay in an area that was free of brush. There were dozens of men moving through the excavations. Most were hunched low and were running. One group went through with each man hanging onto the belt of the man in front of him. Our riflemen were unable to tell how many of these men they hit, but their fire soon caused the Japanese to drop out of sight, perhaps to continue their movements on their hands and knees.

About 7:30 Ernest Thomas paid another short visit to the crater my two friends and I occupied. He told us we would begin attacking at 8:25. There would be a pre-attack bombardment, he said, and we would have tank support when we jumped off.

Thomas asked me whether he could borrow my bayonet. He himself had none, since he was armed with a carbine. I turned mine over to him, wondering why he'd made the request. I'd learn later that he wanted to use it as a pointer while he helped Wells direct the assault.

A group of 3rd Platooners snapped at Camp Pendleton, California, about ten months before the battle. Front row: Keller, Kurelik, Romero. Back row: Lindberg, Wheeler, Lavelle, Adrian, Mooney. Only two of these men (Keller and Mooney) made it through Iwo okay. Two of them (Adrian and Romero) were killed. In the chapter entitled "The Charge," Ed Romero appears twice, once under his own name, and once under the fictitious name "Smith."

My purpose in doing this, when I wrote *Suribachi* in 1965, was to spare Ed Romero's family anguish. Then, some years later I received a letter from a brother of Ed's who did not know I had written the book but had learned that I had been one of Ed's squad-mates. The brother wrote: "In 1945, all we heard from the Marine Corps was that Ed had been killed in action. Ever since, I have been sadly troubled by not knowing exactly what happened to my brother. Can you tell me?" After days of thought (during which I was sternly informed by a longtime professional Marine that, in such cases, you never tell the family the truth), I advised Ed's brother to find a copy of *Suribachi* and read "Smith's" story. The brother soon responded: "Now, at last, I know how Ed went out, and it is a great relief to me. Thank you very much."

Photo by unknown member of 3rd Platoon

As Thomas left, Snyder took his own bayonet from its sheath and fastened it to his rifle.

"You shouldn't have given yours away," he reproved. "You might need it."

"I hope not," I said, repelled by the thought. As long as I had a bullet left I didn't intend to do any bayonet fighting.

The pre-attack bombardment was dominated by the savage efforts of forty carrier-based planes. Many fired rockets that exploded with an ear-splitting sharpness and produced a concussion that seemed to shake the volcano as it might have been shaken by an earthquake. We pulled our heads down when clouds of shrapnel and debris came winging toward our lines.

As the planes made their last run and rumbled away across the water, we knew that our own turn to attack was at hand. And we began to look anxiously toward the rear for our tank support. But there were no tanks on the field. These important machines had again been delayed by refueling and rearming problems. The realization that we'd have to jump off without them made our situation seem even grimmer.

Opening of a 155mm gun is marked by a concussive roar.

Marine Corps Photo

Snyder checked his watch. Then he began to observe our platoon's front line closely. And it wasn't long before Wells climbed out of his crater and signaled, with a sweep of his Thompson, for the rest of us to follow his example. He set off at a trot for Suribachi, and men started to issue from the sand all along our front.

"Okay, let's go," Snyder said quietly. And he, the Indian and I left our crater. The rest of our squad also moved out. We began to trot from hole to hole, pausing in each to catch our breath and scan Suribachi's green fringe for signs of activity. We saw our leading men drag aside the spirals of wire that lay across our path.

For a few moments the hulking fortress remained still. Then it began to react. First came the crack of rifles and the chatter of machine guns. This quickly grew to a heavy rattle, and bullets began to snap and whine about us. Then the mortars started coming, some being visible as they made their high arc, and shortly the area was being blanketed by roaring funnels of steel and sand. The noise and fury increased until our hearing was numbed and our thinking impaired. It was as though the volcano's ancient bowels had suddenly come to life and we were advancing into a full-scale eruption.

Chick Robeson said later of the shelling: "It was terrible, the very worst I can remember our taking. The Jap mortarmen seemed to be playing checkers and using us as their squares. I still can't understand how any of us got through it."

We were now part of a real hell-bent-for-leather attack, the kind the Marines are famous for. But there was nothing inspiring about it. None of our ex-raiders shouted "Gung Ho!"; none of our ex-paratroopers shouted "Geronimo!"; and none of our southerners let go the rebel yell. We felt only reluctance and enervating anxiety. There seemed nothing ahead but death. If we managed somehow to make it across the open area, we'd only become close-range targets for those concealed guns. I myself was seized by a sensation of utter hopelessness. I could feel the fear dragging at my jowls.

It is in situations like this that Marine Corps training proves its value. There probably wasn't a man among us who didn't wish to God he was moving in the opposite direction. But we had been ordered to attack, so we would attack. And our obedience involved more than just a resignation to discipline. Our training had imbued us with a fierce pride in our outfit, and this pride helped now to keep us from faltering. Few of us would have admitted that we were bound by the old-fashioned principle of "death before dishonor," but it was probably this, above all else, that kept us pressing forward.

Men were beginning to fall now, and the cry, "Corpsman! Corpsman!" became a part of the action's mixture of sounds. Raymond Strahm went down a few yards to my left, a piece of shrapnel having pierced his helmet just above his right ear. The helmet slowed the fragment and saved his life (so he could die in the postwar automobile accident mentioned earlier). Pfc. Robert L. Blevins, of

Galesburg, Illinois, next fell with a bullet in the leg. Then a mortar burst killed Corporal Edward J. Romero, Jr., our ex-paratrooper from Chicago.

And then it was my turn.

With shells starting to close in on us, five of us jumped into a huge crater that had probably been formed by a 500-pound bomb dropped by the 7th Air Force. Staying on our feet, we took positions on the forward slope that enabled us to look over the rim toward Suribachi. There was immediately a heavy crash just to our right, and then another a few yards behind us.

Someone said urgently, "Let's get out of here!"

"One place is as bad as another," I countered.

"Yeah," Howard Snyder agreed. "One place is as bad as another."

A moment later a shell exploded, with a fierce lashing of steel and sand and concussion, on our crater's left rim.

My rifle was torn from my hands and I reeled under a hard, ear-ringing blow to the left side of my face. I thought for an instant that I had taken only concussion, but when my hand leapt reflexively to the affected area, the tip of my thumb went through a hole at my jaw line. A fragment had broken my jaw,

A busy moment in the fight for Suribachi.

Defense Dept. Photo

smashed through the roots of two molars and lodged in the muscles beneath my tongue.

Only one man besides me had been hit, and he received but a minor wound in the muscles of his lower back. Because of the way I'll have to discuss this man shortly, I'll give him the fictitious name "Smith."

My own wound started to bleed profusely, both externally and inside my mouth. While Snyder stuck up his head and shouted an urgent call for a

Stunned victim of one of Suribachi's mortar shells.

Defense Dept. Photo

corpsman, I took off my helmet, pack and cartridge belt and sat down against the crater's slope. Spitting out a stream of blood and the crown of a tooth, I wondered worriedly how my injury's two-way flow could be stanched. I was afraid my jugular vein had been hit.

Corpsman Clifford Langley was able to reach me almost at once. He quickly applied compresses, one inside my mouth and one outside, and the bleeding promptly decreased. The inside compress was held in place by my biting down on it, while the other was secured by a bandage that Langley wrapped vertically about my head.

Finishing with me, the corpsman moved across the crater to treat Smith's back.

Now that the emergency was over, Snyder asked whether he could have my pistol, and I was glad to give it to him. He also removed the two fragmentation grenades that were attached to the straps of the pack I'd discarded.

"We'll have to go now," he told me.

"Are we just going to leave him here?" the Indian asked.

"We've got to," Snyder answered. "We'll come back and check on him later."

I could talk, in spite of the bulky compress in my mouth, and I managed to say, "Go fight the war. I'll be okay." Then I added the standard statement for moments like this: "Get a couple for me."

The three unwounded men now climbed out of the crater and pushed on with the attack. Corpsman Langley remained with Smith and me to give us each an injection of morphine. Then he closed his first aid pouch and prepared to go. Deciding it might be wise that he arm himself, even though he was supposed to be a noncombatant, he picked up my rifle, the stock of which I noticed was shrapnel-scarred. He next climbed to the rim of the crater and peered toward Suribachi.

At that moment the crater rocked with another savage, ear-pounding explosion. We had taken a second direct mortar hit.

I let out a sharp involuntary cry as the blast swept over me and tugged heavily at my left calf. My trouser leg, my canvas legging and a large area of skin and flesh had been torn away. The wound was an ugly sight. My calf's major muscle had been laid bare and sliced in two as though by a knife. One of these segments had been pushed slightly to the side, and my first reaction was to reach down and align it with the other.

With my jaw fractured, my blood supply diminished and my calf now severely torn, I felt for an instant that I was nearing death, and I said to myself, aloud, "Well, I guess this is the end." My tone was matter-of-fact. I felt no pain and no particular anguish. The worst had happened, but it really wasn't so terrible after all.

Corpsman Langley was at my side in a moment, and my death vision faded. Langley himself had taken some shrapnel, though I wasn't aware of it at this time. He first sprinkled sulfa on my wound, which wasn't bleeding badly in spite of its seriousness. Then he covered it with an ankle-to-knee battle dressing that fastened along my shin with tie-ties.

As the corpsman finished with me I turned my eyes to Smith and found him to be a tragic sight. Lying on his stomach on the crater's floor, he was now mortally hurt. Both his legs had been horribly lacerated from heel to waist. On his right leg I couldn't see a particle of skin. To make a ghastly but accurate simile: the limb looked like a long pile of raw hamburger.

Smith was the man who had exclaimed apprehensively while we were on our way to the beach, "If only we get in okay!"

Still conscious, he was lying quietly with his head on his folded arms. His face was pale but calm. To make him think that something was being done for him Langley placed a tourniquet, a white cord, around the leg that was most frightfully damaged. The cord contrasted signally with the red flesh it was compressing, and the limb's grisly appearance was heightened.

As the corpsman turned from this measure, he and I had another jarring experience. We heard a heavy thump, and we realized that a third mortar shell had hit the floor of our crater. But this one was a dud. It didn't explode; it merely buried itself. We watched, fearfully fascinated, as sand funneled in over the top of it. Had this shell exploded, we must certainly have been killed.

I now noticed that blood was seeping through the corpsman's clothes at several points, and I asked him whether he wanted me to take a look at his wounds. But he assured me that he wasn't badly hurt. He once more closed his pouch, picked up my rifle and climbed the crater's slope. After sizing up the situation ahead for a few moments, he slipped over the rim and was gone.

Death would soon come to my luckless friend while I sat near him in that evil crater. I would presently be found by stretcher bearers, at which time my brief career as a combat Marine would end. Though I wasn't to be a hero, I had lasted long enough to win an important personal battle. My courage had been put to an extreme test and had held up.

During those moments when Smith's life was slipping away, my own was having a new beginning. Life would seem much sweeter after this. In six months I would be recovered from my wounds, walking without a limp, bearing my scars with pride, enjoying a new confidence. There would seem little to fear after Iwo Jima. I'd know that I'd never be called upon to do anything harder than pit my flesh against Mount Suribachi, however long I lived.

Seeing my years accumulate would bring me more satisfaction than sadness. I'd view gray hairs and wrinkles as the medals that Nature awards to those of us who make it to maturity. As for Death, I had come face to face with that old ogre and had learned that he is mostly sham. I'd enjoy the truce he'd granted me, but would live with the feeling that when he finally renewed his fight in earnest I'd be able to make my surrender without begging for terms.

To return to the attack:

In spite of the continued resistance, a number of our platoon's hole-hopping groups soon neared Suribachi's brush fringe. And they found a degree of hope in the sight of the destruction that had been wrought by our planes and heavy guns. Some of the bunkers and pillboxes whose sand had been blown away had been damaged like the blockhouses we had seen from farther back. Much of the brush had been splintered and denuded, and there were patches that had been seared black by napalm flames.

But as our men began to rush the first defenses they discovered that there were still plenty of live defenders among them.

Hank Hansen and Donald Ruhl, who had been charging in the lead with Wells, ran to the top of a silent pillbox and promptly clashed with a unit of Japanese in a network of trenches just behind it. While the two Marines were emptying their rifles at these men, a demolitions charge came flying through the air and landed in front of them.

Ruhl hollered, "Look out, Hank!" and dived on the charge and absorbed its full blast.

Stretcher team making an emergency rescue.

Photo by Lou Lowery

Hansen, recoiling back off the pillbox, was spattered with blood and bits of flesh. With the mound between him and the enemy, he reached up and grabbed Ruhl by the foot.

Wells, who was crouching nearby, quickly ordered, "Leave him alone. He's dead." The lieutenant had seen Ruhl's arm fly back and reveal a gory cavity where his chest had been.

Donald Ruhl, our platoon malcontent, the target of our criticism, had sacrificed himself to save a comrade. And for his deed he would be awarded the Congressional Medal of Honor.

Howard Snyder and his men were moving up on the left flank of the pillbox now, and they took up the fight. Our squad had started from the reserve spot twenty-five yards behind the others, and had lost three men to mortar fire, but our aggressive little leader had managed to move the rest up fast.

The Japanese had begun to scurry back and forth through the trenches, and they were jabbering excitedly. They seemed to be trying to organize for a counterattack.

Snyder and Harold Keller quickly began to lob hand grenades among them, and Chick Robeson and Louie Adrian took turns at firing with their BARs.

Tagging a casualty for evacuation.

Defense Dept. Photo

One man would stand up and shoot until he'd emptied his weapon; then the other would jump up and the first would duck to reload.

After Snyder and Keller had thrown all the grenades the squad was carrying, Wells tossed them his own and ordered more passed up to them. The two ex-raiders threw so many of the heavy missiles at this point that they wore their fingers sore. But the combination of grenades and BAR bullets took its toll of the scampering enemy, and no counterattack developed.

But now Louie Adrian, while standing erect and firing into the trenches, took a bullet in the chest. His BAR kept chugging as he crumpled to the sand.

Snyder stooped over him, took a look at the wound and said with a frown, "He's gone." The bullet had pierced the Indian's stout young heart.

Adrian's death came as a severe shock to Chick Robeson. He said afterward: "We had met when we enlisted in Spokane, and we had been together constantly for fourteen months. Seeing him die so suddenly is something I'll never forget. He wasn't only my friend; he was my link with home."

Covered by two riflemen, a flamethrower operator sends a blast through a pillbox entrance. This nondescript pile of sand is a typical Iwo Jima pillbox. The sand often conceals a cubicle of masonry.

Defense Dept. Photo

Harold Keller was paternally concerned about Chick's welfare even during these tense moments, and he ordered the youth away from the body.

Only a short time before, the Indian had been worrying about leaving me wounded in a bomb crater. Now he himself was dead. He had been shot through the jacket I had lent him the preceding evening, and he'd be buried in it.

When our squad had come ashore, Snyder had nine men under him. Now he had but three: Harold Keller, Chick Robeson and Phil Christman. And Christman was bearing wounds from the grenade that had got Ed Kurelik.

By this time our platoon's second and third squads, led by Bob Lane and Katie Midkiff, had moved in among the leading attackers, and one of Midkiff's BAR men, big Leo Rozek, hurried forward and took up the firing.

Our company had advanced faster than the company on its right, and Wells shortly realized that our platoon was taking fire not only from the front but from the flank. He found it necessary to send Ernest Thomas over to contact the lagging unit and make an urgent request for support.

Now a Marine carrying a light machine gun moved into the platoon's zone, and the lieutenant placed him on the line. He began to make it hot for the entrenched Japanese, but he was soon shot dead. Several other men tried to operate the gun, but they were all shot away from it. The gun itself took multiple hits and was damaged.

During these moments a bunker that lay just ahead of the platoon began to emit a dispersion of hand grenades. Many of our men were pinned down by these blasts, and there wasn't much could be done about them. Rifle fire proved ineffective, and the platoon was out of grenades of its own; and Chuck Lindberg's assault squad, with its flamethrowers and demolitions, hadn't yet made its final break through the mortar fire that was still being laid on the open sand.

Corporal Wayne C. Hathaway, a quiet-spoken ex-raider from El Dorado, Kansas, volunteered to go back for grenades, and Wells consented to the mission. Hathaway took with him Private Edward Krisik, an eighteen-year-old Milwaukee youth who was seeing his first action. But the pair hadn't gone far before they were shot down. Both were wounded fatally, Hathaway taking a dumdum bullet that tore up his insides.

Several members of the assault squad had got through the shellfire with demolitions now, and Hank Hansen told Wells he thought he could get to the bunker with a charge.

The lieutenant says of this: "I told him to try it, because we weren't getting anywhere trying to dodge those damned grenades. He took a large demolitions satchel and put in a time fuse. Then he ran at the bunker. But instead of placing the charge at an aperture he threw it—and missed. We all had to duck, because when that C-2 composition went off it rocked the whole area. The dirt had hardly settled before grenades were flying like mad."

To make matters worse, Suribachi's mortarmen had begun to pull in some of their fire, and shells were starting to burst alarmingly close. The trajectory of the missiles was high, and some could be seen coming. A direct hit was soon scored on an amphibian tractor that was trying to reach the platoon with supplies.

One of our company's communications men now ran up to Wells with a telephone whose wire trailed across the sand toward the rear. And the lieutenant, lying in a depression with several of his men, made a report of the platoon's situation to Captain Severance. Wells looked rearward while phoning and saw our intrepid battalion commander, Colonel Johnson, standing conspicuously on a knoll not far behind the action. He was watching it through binoculars. It was at this time that our platoon became the colonel's favorite. He had a fighting heart himself, and he liked the unhesitating way our men had rushed Suribachi's guns.

Chuck Lindberg had brought up the rest of the assault squad by this time, and Wells prepared to direct our two flamethrower men against the bunker and the other busy defenses. But the effort was impeded by mortar fire, which now had the platoon's range.

One of the shells soon scored a bull's-eye. It burst among Wells, Bob Lane, Pappy Lavelle, Dick White and Pfc. William S. Wayne. All five were wounded. Wells was hit hard along the back of both legs, Lane took a fragment in the shoulder—and a big one in his helmet, Lavelle was struck in the hand, White received severe lower leg and foot injuries and Wayne took scattered hits.

Wells had been lying on his stomach, facing the front, and the shell had landed just behind him. He says of the experience: "It went off right at my feet. When the dust cleared I heard Dick White say he'd lost a heel. I saw Howard Snyder looking down at me like he thought I was a goner. I had no feeling below the waist, and a burning sensation in my neck. When I reached down and felt my legs I found them all wet. I thought it was all blood, but a piece of shrapnel had exploded one of my canteens. My clothes were nearly all blown off me from the waist down, and I was full of shrapnel."

But the lieutenant didn't relinquish his command. By the time Corpsman John Bradley had given him first aid and had injected him with morphine the feeling had crept back into his legs. And, learning that he could still move, he disregarded his wounds and turned his attention once more to the platoon's problems.

The situation had become critical. Since the start of the attack our unit had lost seventeen men, over a third of its number. We had jumped off with forty-two. There were now only twenty-five left. These were extremely high losses for only forty-five minutes of action—high enough to raise the threat of disorganization and panic. And our men were still being taxed to the limit of their endurance and had only a precarious hold on the section of line they had hit.

But then things began to look up. Braving the mortar shells, hand grenades and small-arms fire, Chuck Lindberg and Private Robert D. Goode, a muscular Californian, started to move against the bunker and the other defenses with their flamethrowers. Our riflemen covered them by shooting at the menacing apertures. The results the two men achieved were dramatic—and terrible. Squirting streams of fire at every opening they could find, they began to destroy dozens of the enemy. The bunker and the pillboxes were turned into furnaces. Their ammunition was exploded, and shell casings, bullet casings, hand grenade fragments and other pieces of debris came flying out through the smoking apertures.

As the Japanese died, the platoon could smell their roasting flesh. And some of our men said later that the circumstances made the odor seem the sweetest they had ever smelled.

Chuck Lindberg earned the Silver Star at this point. Though he knew he was a conspicuous target with the bulky flamethrower tank on his back,

When the author was evacuated from Iwo Jima the afternoon of the day he was wounded, he was placed on a hospital ship about a mile offshore, and he thought he was safe. But that evening our fleet was hit by 25 kamikazes (suicide planes) that were after our aircraft carriers. The *Saratoga* (shown here) lost 300 men killed and wounded, and was so badly damaged it had to head for Pearl Harbor. The *Bismarck Sea* was sunk with a loss of more than 300 dead. Three other vessels were damaged. All of the Japanese attackers died.

Official Navy Photo

he moved among the defenses as though they were training-field dummies. Robert Leader, one of those who watched Chuck work and felt a great wave of relief at his violent accomplishments, later referred to his performance as "a remarkable example of cool-headed fighting."

Tanks were moving up all along the line now, and the assault on the first defenses became assured of success. As tank crews and infantrymen, working together, began to drive wedges into the belt of bunkers and pillboxes, the mutual-support arrangement of the fortifications was disrupted and their resistance began to diminish. And the survivors of the trench fighting were forced to fall back to positions nearer the volcano's base.

During this phase of the action our tattered and bloody lieutenant was still directing the platoon's attack, and he was almost hit again, this time by machine gun fire. He was moving on the platoon's left flank when the die-hard gunner opened up. With bullets cracking past him, Wells hobbled to a reduced pillbox and dropped behind it.

The gunner was in the open, and he was shortly spotted by a BAR man belonging to Lieutenant Pennell's 2nd Platoon, which was operating on our unit's left. A duel resulted.

Wells soon heard someone shout, "You got him, Lew!"

This was followed by a sadder announcement: "Yes, and he got me."

Wells learned later that the Marine and the Japanese died almost simultaneously.

In his fall behind the pillbox the lieutenant had got his wounds full of sand, and they now began to pain him severely. Corpsman Bradley came to him and gave him a second shot of morphine and also made an attempt to clean and re-dress the wounds. The Corpsman told Wells sternly that he ought to head for the rear at once and have himself properly treated.

But the lieutenant stayed at the front for another half hour. Then, finally deciding that he was no longer fit to command, he turned the platoon over to Ernest Thomas and started to crawl to the rear on his hands and knees. The trip was long, tiring and perilous, but he managed at length to reach an aid station. From there he was transported by stretcher to the beach, and a landing craft soon took him from the island.

For his work that morning our lieutenant was awarded the Navy Cross. He received the high-ranking medal, his citation stated, "for extraordinary hero-ism against the enemy while he was serving as a rifle platoon leader in a Marine infantry battalion on Iwo Jima.

"When he was ordered to attack across open terrain and dislodge the enemy from a series of strongly defended pillboxes and blockhouses at the base of Mount Suribachi, 1st Lieutenant Wells courageously and without regard for his personal safety placed himself in the forefront of his platoon and led his men forward in the face of intense hostile machine gun, mortar and rifle fire, continuously moving from one flank to the other, leading assault groups one by one in their attacks on enemy emplacements, encouraging and exhorting his men to greater efforts.

"While personally leading his demolitions squad in an assault on a formidable blockhouse whose fire had stopped the advance of his platoon he was severely wounded, yet he continued to lead the assault until the blockhouse was destroyed.

"An hour later, when the pain from his wounds became so great that he could no longer walk, he established his command post in such a position that he could observe the forward progress of his men, whose attack he continued to control for one half hour more by means of messengers.

"By his exceptionally heroic leadership he so inspired his men that they destroyed at least twenty-five emplacements. His indomitable fighting spirit, great personal valor and exemplary devotion to duty were in keeping with the highest traditions of the United States Naval Service."

Our lieutenant had proved himself a remarkable man. We had hit the beach with doubts about him, but he had ended up winning our utmost admiration.

Beach scene in Mount Suribachi area on February 23, the day the flag was raised. This is a remarkable depiction of the dangerous troop-congestion problem the invaders experienced.

Marine Corps Photo

It's true that he didn't spare our blood to achieve the objective. But this is the kind of military leadership that gets things done. And in the long run it actually saves lives.

When twenty-year-old Ernest Thomas took over the platoon he began to lead it with the same spirit Wells had shown. And he personally directed tanks against several pillboxes and caves that proved too hot for our men to handle. It was he who discovered the soft spot in the belt of defenses that enabled our battalion to begin a relentless, death-dealing drive toward the volcano's base. He himself led the breakthrough.

During our training days I had seen Thomas blanch, as many men do, when he was required to take an injection. But on the battlefield, when he was at every moment risking a real perforation, he seemed dauntless.

Thomas, too, won the coveted Navy Cross. Colonel Johnson approached him after the breakthrough and told him the recommendation would be made. Though Thomas wouldn't live to accept the award, he would die knowing he had it coming.

Since the jump-off, our platoon had earned a Medal of Honor, two Navy Crosses, a Silver Star and seventeen Purple Hearts. This is a considerable list of decorations to come to one rifle platoon in a couple of hours of battle. In fact, our showing probably stands as the best that any Marine Corps platoon has ever achieved in an assault of this nature.

TO THE SUMMIT WITH
THE FLAG

Up to this time our regiment had been taking more punishment than it had been dealing, but now it began to strike back with a vengeance. Its three battalions hammered fiercely at the semicircle of defenses, destroying the enemy in growing numbers and pressing ever closer to the volcano's base.

Our rifle companies had plenty of help. Constantly busy with demolitions were elements of the 5th Engineer Battalion. These men sometimes forgot they belonged to a support unit and took on bunkers, pillboxes and caves that lay out ahead of the front lines. Also continuing their vigorous aid were the regiment's tanks, howitzers, halftracks and 37-millimeter guns. Assisting from the air were alert observation planes, and lying close offshore were ships that fired when notified of targets. Supply lines to the front were maintained by amphibian vehicles and men on foot.

The two-day assault on the fortifications was accompanied by a sustained din. Only our flamethrowers wrought their slaughter quietly. They went into action with a metallic click and a long whoosh. But these were no doubt the most terrifying sounds the Japanese heard.

Hand-to-hand fighting sometimes resulted when enemy soldiers would suddenly dart from cover to attack or to make a break for the safety of more remote defenses. There were a number of bayonetings and knife killings. One Marine, attacked by a saber-swinging Japanese officer, caught the blade with his bare hands, wrested it from the man and hacked him to death with it. I saw this Marine later when he was brought aboard the hospital ship I occupied a mile or two offshore. He stopped by my bunk and told me his story. Both his hands were badly gashed and were swathed in bandages—but he still had the Japanese sword.

In a six-photo sequence, Lou Lowery tells the story of the capture of one of the defenders of the Suribachi sector.

Marine interpreter with Japanese soldier who has been wounded and partly buried by an artillery burst. The man was found during a Marine advance into a Japanese position that had been "softened up" by heavy shellfire.

Japanese soldier signals with his fingers that he'd like a cigarette.

Interpreter gives enemy soldier a puff from the cigarette he'd been smoking himself.

Marines carry prisoner to an aid station.

American doctor examines prisoner and learns that his wounds are not serious, that he is suffering mostly from shock.

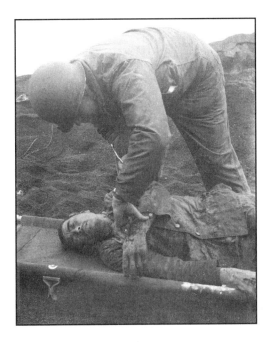

Revived prisoner is interrogated by interpreter.

Several organized counterattacks were launched, but each was soon broken up. It isn't likely that the Japanese expected to accomplish much with these measures, but charging the advancing Marines was a way of death that many doubtless preferred to being exterminated in their failing defenses.

At one time during the bloody activities a Marine officer who could speak Japanese took a loud-speaker into the front lines and called upon Suribachi's surviving defenders to lay down their arms and surrender. But the appeal was ignored.

Attacking on the extreme left, the 3rd Platoon and the other units of Easy Company reached the volcano's base on the afternoon of the first day. They next sliced around its left flank. Once they had reached the area where the defenses thinned, they were ordered by Colonel Johnson to dig in and hold.

A similar attack was made by the 1st Battalion on the right. But in the center, where the 3rd Battalion was operating, going was tougher. An extra day was required for these units to batter their way to the base.

By the end of D-plus-3 the fight was largely won. There were still substantial numbers of the enemy in caves and other places of concealment, but hundreds had been slain and the pernicious power of the fortress had been broken.

It was time for the regiment to start climbing. But the craggy 550-foot dome was so steep that a cooperative move could not be made. It was discovered that the only route to the crater lay in the 2nd Battalion zone, so the job of planning the climb fell to Colonel Johnson. And he soon decided to send one of his rifle platoons up as an assault patrol.

The twenty-five men of the 3rd Platoon were by this time, very dirty and very tired. They no longer looked nor felt like crack combat troops. Although they'd just had a relatively free day their rest had been marred by a chilling rain. They hardly yearned for the distinction of being the first Marines to tackle the volcano. But the colonel didn't bother to ask them how they felt about it.

By this time our unit had more than proved its combat capability. It almost seemed as though our high-spirited lieutenant had been granted the fifty men he'd wished for in training—the fifty who weren't afraid to die and could take any position.

About 8:00 o'clock on the morning of D-plus-4 Lieutenant Harold Schrier, our company executive officer, assembled the platoon. After its thin ranks had been bolstered by replacements from other Easy Company units, he led it back around the volcano to 2nd Battalion headquarters near the northeast base.

The men found our dynamic battalion commander standing outside an improvised pup tent sipping from a cup of steaming coffee. He was wearing his fatigue cap with its visor bent upward, and this gave him a jaunty appearance that belied his stern nature. He was smiling this morning, however, so he must have been pleased with the way things were going.

While Johnson and Harold Schrier consulted, the men were issued an abundant replenishment of cartridges, hand grenades, demolitions and flame thrower fuel. They were also provided large water cans from which they filled their canteens. During these preparations they were joined by a radioman, two teams of stretcher bearers and a photographer, Staff Sergeant Louis R. Lowery of *Leatherneck* magazine.

As the forty-man patrol loaded up to move out, the colonel handed Schrier a folded American flag that had been brought ashore by our battalion adjutant, 1st Lieutenant George G. Wells. He had been carrying it in his map case. The

Scene at headquarters of 2nd Battalion, 28th Marines, as the 3rd Platoon of Easy Company gets orders to tackle Suribachi's summit. Colonel Chandler Johnson, on telephone, is asking that all naval gunfire on the volcano be lifted. Standing with Johnson, left to right, are Howard Snyder, Harold Schrier, and Harold Keller.

Photo by Lou Lowery, courtesy of Vi Lindberg

flag had been obtained from the *Missoula,* the transport that had borne our battalion to Saipan, our staging area.

Johnson's orders were simple. The patrol was to climb to the summit, secure the crater and raise the flag. Though our men hoped fervently that their mission would prove as uncomplicated as the colonel made it sound, most had serious misgivings.

Harold Keller said later: "When I looked at the two stretchers that were being sent along, I thought to myself, 'We'll probably need a hell of a lot more than that.' "

However, Johnson had earlier sent two small patrols up the dome on reconnoitering missions, and both had reached the rim of the crater and had then withdrawn without running into any trouble.

Falling into an irregular column, our men headed directly for the volcano's base. They moved briskly at first, soon passing a Marine howitzer that had taken a direct hit from an enemy gun in the north. There were two dead men lying by the weapon. A little farther on they passed several enemy corpses, one of which was wearing bright orange shoes.

When the route turned steep and going became difficult, the lieutenant sent out flankers to guard the vulnerable column against surprise attack. Heavily laden with weapons and ammunition, the men climbed slowly and were forced to stop from time to time to catch their breath. Some areas were so steep they had to be negotiated on hands and knees. Though several cave entrances were sighted, no resistance developed.

Far below, the Marines located about the northeast base watched the patrol's laborious ascent. Also observing, some through binoculars, were many men of the fleet.

Within a half hour after leaving battalion headquarters the patrol reached the crater's rim. Schrier called a halt here while he took stock of the situation. He could see two or three battered gun emplacements and some cave entrances, but there were no Japanese in evidence. So he gave the signal for the men to start filing over.

My bold friend Howard Snyder went over first. Had I remained unwounded I probably would have been second—whether I wanted to be or not. As it was, Harold Keller occupied this spot. Chick Robeson was third. Then came Harold Schrier, his radioman and Leo Rozek. Robert Leader was seventh, and, fully expecting to be fired at, he hoped that number seven was really the lucky number it was supposed to be.

As the men entered the crater they fanned out and took up positions just inside the rim. They were tensed for action, but the rim caves and the yawning reaches below them remained silent. Finally one of the men stood up and urinated down the crater's slope. But even this insulting gesture didn't bring the Japanese to life.

Japanese dead at Suribachi's base. The pair had apparently been shot down while running for the shelter of a cave.

Photo by Lou Lowery

Charred body of a flamethrower victim.

Photo by Lou Lowery

Ascending patrol passes silenced gun emplacement.

Photo by Lou Lowery

Flag is displayed for a camera shot.

Photo by Lou Lowery

Marine with carbine covering left flank of patrol as it nears Suribachi's crater rim. Starkly illustrated is the threat posed by the volcano to the landing beaches.

Photo by Lou Lowery

Ernest Thomas on the alert as the rim is reached.

Photo by Lou Lowery

While half the patrol stayed at the rim, the other half now began to press into the crater to probe for resistance and to look for something that could be used as a flagpole.

Harold Keller, moving in the lead, made the first contact with the enemy. He says of this: "The Jap started to climb out of a deep hole, his back toward me. I fired three times from the hip, and he dropped out of sight."

Several caves now began to disgorge hand grenades. The Marines in the hot spots took cover and replied with grenades of their own. Some of these came flying back out of the dark entrances before exploding.

Even while this action waxed, Robert Leader and Leo Rozek discovered a long piece of pipe, seemingly a remnant of a raincatching system, and passed it to the summit. Waiting with the flag were Harold Schrier, Ernest Thomas, Hank Hansen and Chuck Lindberg. They promptly began fixing it to the pole.

It was about 10:30 A.M. when the pole was planted and the Stars and Stripes, seized by the wind, began to whip proudly over the volcano. The date February 23, 1945, had suddenly become historically significant. Mount Suribachi was the first piece of Japanese-owned territory—not counting mandates like Saipan—to be captured by American forces during World War II.

The Marines watching from below raised the cry, "There goes the flag!" And the electrifying word quickly spread to all the units about the volcano's base and to the regiments fighting the main battle to the north. Our combat-weary troops felt a great swell of pride and exultation. They felt a certain relief too. A part of the "impregnable" island had fallen. Victory seemed a little nearer now. Some men cheered, and some wiped at brimming eyes.

The cry was also taken up by the fleet. Ship whistles tooted a spirited salute. Aboard my hospital ship I thrilled to the news as it came over the public address system—though I wasn't aware at the time that it was my own platoon that had raised the flag.

Word of the achievement would also soon be heartening the people at home, who had been following the progress of the battle anxiously, dismayed by the reports of our mounting casualties.

Photographer Lou Lowery snapped the flag raising from a hole where he crouched with BAR man Chick Robeson. Chick had been urged to join the flag-raising group for the picture but had refused, insisting that he was no "Hollywood Marine." In addition to the four flag raisers—Schrier, Thomas, Hansen and Lindberg—also identifiable on the photo is Pfc. James R. Michels, the man on guard in the foreground.

Though most of our men were aware of the significance of their accomplishment, no one at first did much thinking in terms of pride and glory. All were concerned about the effect the sight of the colors would have on the enemy. They were in danger of getting resistance not only from the Japanese close at hand but from artillery units in the north. The forty men had raised the flag, but they were by no means certain they would be able to defend it successfully.

Shells from the north wouldn't come until later, but the flag was promptly challenged by the Japanese on the summit. First a rifleman stepped out of a cave and fired at the photographer and Chick Robeson. The Japanese missed, but

Mysterious John Bradley.

This Lou Lowery photo shows a group from the 3rd Platoon's patrol preparing to raise the first flag. John Bradley, later to become famous as one of the second raisers, is the man in the center, his back to the camera, his corpman gear evident.

After the war, Bradley is known to have lamented repeatedly that he and the other men in the famous Rosenthal photo got entirely too much undeserved attention.

In 1960 the author telephoned Bradley, his old platoon-mate, and explained that he was planning to do a book giving the 3rd Platoon's flag-raising story its rightful place in history. The author asked: "Will you help me with this?"

Bradley responded: "No, I'm too busy." The author was never again in touch with Bradley, and the mystery remains unsolved.

Robeson didn't. He swung his BAR up for a long burst, and the man dropped heavily.

"You got him!" Harold Schrier said.

The body was quickly seized by the feet and dragged part way back into the cave. But now an officer stepped out. Grimacing bitterly, he charged toward the flag-raising group brandishing a sword that had only half a blade. He had probably broken the weapon on purpose so it would have no value as a souvenir.

First flag-raising as snapped for *Leatherneck* magazine by Marine Corps combat photographer, Lou Lowery.

There are at least eight men in this photo, only four of whom are readily identifiable: Sergeant Henry O. Hansen (without helmet); Platoon Sergeant Ernest I. Thomas (hand on knee); Pfc. James R. Michels (on guard); and Corporal Charles W. Lindberg (behind Michels). One of those obscured by the seated Thomas, besides Lieutenant Harold Schrier, might well be John Bradley, famous for his second-raising role. And, at this writing at the close of 2006, Pfc. Raymond Jacobs is making a notably credible bid for recognition as the radioman on the left.

Chuck Lindberg, who had just helped raise the flag, looks for cave entrances along crater's rim.

Photo by Lou Lowery

Kenneth Espenes and Howard Snyder check out a cave system while the newly raised flag flies at upper right.

Photo by Lou Lowery, courtesy of Jon Espenes

Howard Snyder advanced to meet this attack with the .45 pistol I had given him. He took deliberate aim as the frenzied man bore down. But when he pressed the trigger there was only a metallic snap. The weapon misfired.

Snyder had to scramble out of the way, but a dozen Marines were now alerted to the cave threat. A volley of rifle fire, led off by Pfc. Clarence H. Garrett, turned the one-man charge into a headlong tumble.

Our men now moved against the resisting area, and they were met by a flurry of hand grenades. The cave turned out to be a large one with several entrances.

Flanking the openings, the Marines once more countered with grenades of their own. Then the entrances were hosed with flamethrowers and blown shut with demolitions.

Photographer Lowery, covering the action at considerable risk, soon had another close shave. A Japanese lobbed a grenade at him, and he was forced to leap down the side of the volcano. Tumbling for fifty feet before he was able to catch hold of a bush, he broke his camera.

This cave was a far greater threat to the flag raisers than was realized at the time. Howard Snyder and Chick Robeson would make the discovery a few days later, when they dug the cave open to look for souvenirs.

Marine at far left is examining body of enemy officer shot while lunging from cave. Other two Marines are alert for further trouble. Shortly after taking this picture, Lou Lowery, obliged to dodge a hand grenade, tumbled fifty feet down outside slope of volcano, breaking his camera but saving his film.

Robeson says of the venture: "The stench that met us was so foul that we had to put on gas masks. We went in with a small flashlight, and we found it to be a large cave in two parts. Dead Japs lay all about, so thick that we had to tread on some. I believe there were at least 150. Many had held hand grenades to their stomachs, I suppose after we had sealed them in. We found souvenirs galore, and also some maps and papers that we turned over to Schrier. But we really caught hell for being so stupid, and the cave was blown shut a second time—so completely that no darned fools could try such a trick again."

Why these Japanese hadn't tried to bolt from the cave and overwhelm the flag-raising patrol is a mystery. They had our men outnumbered four-to-one. What makes the situation even more unaccountable is that there were other occupied caves on the summit. The number of Japanese who could have hurled themselves against the patrol will never be known, but there were surely enough to have killed every man in it.

Other platoons soon joined the patrol at the summit and began to help with the crater mop-up. Similar operations were still going on at the volcano's base and had also been started on its outer slopes.

Two hours after the flag was raised, Colonel Johnson ordered it seized as a battalion trophy. Moreover, it measured only fifty-four by twenty-eight inches, and it was lost to distant view. Since the sight of the colors was important to the morale of our troops, who still had a lot of fighting to do before Iwo was secured, Johnson felt that a larger set was needed. So a flag that was eight feet by four-feet-eight-inches was obtained from LST 779, a vessel beached near Suribachi's eastern base.

As the new flag was being carried up the volcano, Joe Rosenthal, a civilian photographer who was covering the Iwo operation for the Associated Press, learned of the move and decided to follow. And this decision resulted in the now-famous photograph—the photograph that pushed the 3rd Platoon's heroic story into the background and rendered our flag raisers nameless. Although about half the platoon was present at the second raising, only one of our men, Corpsman John Bradley, is on Rosenthal's picture.

So much has been written about the second event that it needn't be discussed here. But this much ought to be said: the photograph deserves to be popular; it depicts an authentic combat scene, even though the circumstances were less impromptu and dangerous than those of the earlier raising.

There is an interesting footnote to the Suribachi story. When Lieutenant Wells learned, aboard his hospital ship, that it was his platoon that had raised the flag over the volcano, he refused to remain a casualty. He talked a doctor into supplying him with a first aid kit full of morphine and sulfa, and he hitched a ride ashore in a press boat. Limping painfully to Suribachi, he was met at its base by Chuck Lindberg and Bob Goode, who carried him to the summit. There he enjoyed a warm reunion with his men. And in spite of a

This photo shows the small flag, which was first raised on Mount Suribachi, being replaced about two hours later by the large flag that became famous. The exchange was made while combat conditions still prevailed. Joe Rosenthal, of the Associated Press, took his famous photo a few seconds before this one was taken—while the big flag was on its way up. This photo shows the raisers trying to secure their pole among the rocks.

By Marine combat photographer Bob Campbell

The famous Associated Press photo by Joe Rosenthal—a flag replacement that came to symbolize the Battle of Iwo Jima and American courage everywhere. These men were all members of Easy Company, but John Bradley (conspicuous in the center) is the only one who was part of the original 3rd Platoon patrol.

fuming telephone protest from Colonel Johnson, he reassumed command of the platoon and directed the rest of its mop-up operations.

By the time Mount Suribachi was finally declared secured, the 28th Marines had lost about nine hundred men. But the grimmest part of the tale is that our regiment's ordeal was only beginning. The unit was alerted for its move to the northern front on D-plus-9.

Lieutenant Wells tried to go along north with the 3rd Platoon, but he didn't get very far.

Chick Robeson says of this: "Colonel Johnson caught him and really gave him hell. I'll always remember the way we marched off in a double column with Wells standing between us and grabbing each of us emotionally, almost in tears because he had to stay behind. He was truly a great Marine."

In spite of his wounds, Wells managed to remain on the island until it was secured. Thus he became technically a veteran of the entire battle.

During its twenty-five days in the north, the 28th contributed much to the battle's success. But the numberless northern defenses proved every bit as tough as Suribachi's, and our valiant combat team was cut to pieces. Among the many officers killed was Colonel Johnson, who advanced into a shellburst that literally blew him apart.

As for the 3rd Platoon, it was virtually wiped out. Nineteen more of our men were killed or wounded, and two suffered combat fatigue. Our casualty rate for the whole operation was a staggering 91 percent.

The four men who made it through the battle were Harold Keller, James Michels (who took a minor wound that he disregarded), Graydon Dyce and Private Philip L. Ward. Pfc. Manuel Panizo came close to making it; he was wounded on the last day.

Our young platoon sergeant, Ernest Thomas, Navy Cross winner and flag raiser, was fatally shot while trying to summon tank aid to get our men out of a tight spot. His death seemed particularly sad because he was a brilliant, personable youth who appeared destined for high achievement.

Among the slain were also: flag raiser Hank Hansen, the man Donald Ruhl had sacrificed himself to save; Katie Midkiff, who had fretted wryly in training about being one of our lieutenant's fifty men who weren't afraid to die; and my good friend and fearless example, Howard Snyder, who had looked forward to the landing—and to returning safely to his pretty bride. His death ended a friendship we had both counted on continuing after the war.

Chuck Lindberg, flag raiser and Silver Star winner, finally had to lay down his devastating flamethrower when he caught a bullet in the forearm. He withdrew from the field shaking the fist of his good arm at the concealed sniper.

BAR man Chick Robeson was shot in the hand while exposing himself to cover Corpsman Bradley and a man he was treating under fire. The bullet shattered two of Chick's fingers.

Our Massachusetts art student, Robert Leader, was shot through the middle while advancing on a bunker with a hand grenade. Harold Keller managed to drag him to safety, and he survived the critical wound to become a well-known liturgical artist and chair of the art department at the University of Notre Dame.

Ex-raider Keller, the only one of our noncoms to get through unhurt, had to be especially lucky to make it, since he was repeatedly in the fore of the action. But he says casually of his escape: "After I got hit on Bougainville, I guess there were just no more Jap bullets with my name on them."

This, then, is the way it was with the 3rd Platoon of Company E, 2nd Battalion, 28th Marines. It is my earnest hope that these pages will win my former comrades some of the attention they deserve. Not only were they Iwo Jima's real flag-raising heroes, but they probably showed as much spirit in battle as any comparable group in American history. I am very proud to have served with them.

Men like these—men with fighting hearts and boundless courage—are still one of our country's greatest assets. Let us hope there will always be enough of their kind to rally to the flag when its glory is threatened.

Roster of the 3rd Platoon, Company E, 2nd Battalion, 28th Marines, 5th Marine Division, as of February 19, 1945.

First Lieutenant John K. Wells
Platoon Sergeant Ernest I. Thomas
Sergeant Henry O. Hansen (Platoon Guide)

1st Squad
Sergeant Howard M. Snyder
Corporal Harold P. Keller
Corporal Edward J. Romero, Jr.
Corporal Richard J. Wheeler
Pfc. Louie B. Adrian
Pfc. Phillip E. Christman
Pfc. John J. Fredotovich
Pfc. Edward S. Kurelik
Pfc. James A. Robeson
Pfc. Raymond A. Strahm

3rd Squad
Sergeant Kenneth D. Midkiff
Corporal James E. Hagstrom
Corporal Robert A. Leader
Pfc. Graydon W. Dyce
Pfc. Bert M. Freedman
Pfc. Leo J. Rozek
Pvt. Kenneth S. Espenes
Pvt. Clark L. Gaylord
Pvt. Ralph A. Ignatowski
Pvt. John G. Scheperle
Pvt. Charles E. Schott

2nd Squad
Corporal Robert M. Lane
Corporal Wayne C. Hathaway
Corporal Everett M. Lavelle
Pfc. Robert L. Blevins
Pfc. Alva E. Jefferson
Pfc. Manuel Panizo
Pfc. Donald J. Ruhl
Pfc. William S. Wayne
Pvt. James D. Breitenstein
Pvt. Ogle T. Lemon

Assault Squad
Corporal Charles W. Lindberg
Pfc. John H. Eller
Pfc. Clarence H. Garrett
Pfc. Clarence R. Hipp
Pfc. William J. McNulty
Pfc. James R. Michels
Pfc. Richard S. White
Pvt. Robert D. Goode
Pvt. Edward Krisik
Pvt. Philip L. Ward

Navy Hospital Corpsmen
PhM2c John H. Bradley
PhM3c Clifford R. Langley

AFTERWORD

The Essence of Iwo Jima in a Nutshell of Rhymes

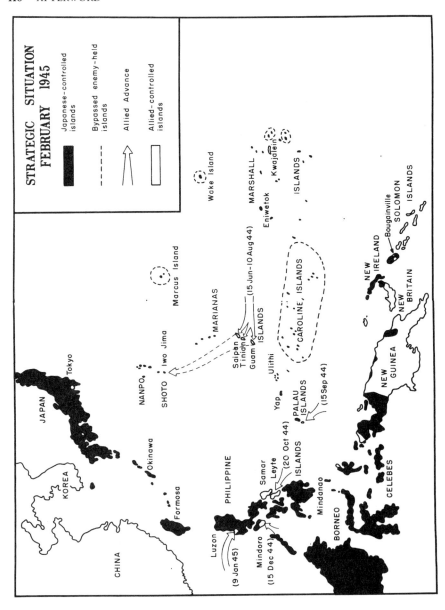

STRATEGIC SITUATION
FEBRUARY 1945

Japanese-controlled islands

Bypassed enemy-held islands

Allied Advance

Allied-controlled islands

SEA CHANGE

A smidgen in
The blue Pacific,
South of
Motherland Japan,
Iwo Jima
Lay aslumber
Till mighty
World War Two began.

An urgent need
For island airstrips
Became a feature
Of the game,
And tiny Iwo,
Now strategic,
Awoke to
Everlasting fame.

THE UNDERGROUND TROOPS
(1944)

Before the fight
The Japanese
Put all their works
Beneath the ground.
They widened caves,
Dug tunnels too,
And planted bunkers,
Mound by mound.

But even as
They plied their tools
And barracked in
Their secret rooms,
They understood
That, in the end,
Their sunken works
Would be their tombs.

FULLY PREPARED

The fleet that bore
The trained Marines,
Who had their orders
To proceed,
Held countless tons
Of martial stores,
Supplies to fill
Their every need.

This bounty made
For confidence,
But shadows marked
A certain fact:
Included with
The laden goods
Were wooden crosses,
Thickly stacked.

The Fifth Division's crosses on display. The cemetery, however, will be occupied only until the dead can be taken home.

Photo by Lou Lowery

THE SAMURAI SWORD

This weapon of
The Japanese
Was long revered
In song and story
As symbolizing
Martial things
That magnified
Their nation's glory.

But those who bore
The sword on Iwo
Could not advance
Its proud traditions.
The modern foe
Was primed to fight
With raging flames
And demolitions.

GETTING ASHORE
(February 19, 1945)

The shoreline chosen
For the landing
Was not too difficult
To reach.
By plan, the foe
Withheld their fire
Till men were thick
Upon the beach.

Then heavy guns
Began to roar,
And lighter arms
Began to crack.
Although entrapped,
The staunch Marines
Prepared at once
For fighting back.

MOUNT SURIBACHI
(February 23, 1945)

Iwo Jima's
Dead volcano
Was brought to life
By pulsing guns.
The storming troops
Were grimly thinned,
And yet they mastered
Nippon's sons.

At last a flag
Adorned the summit,
A vantage point
Supremely prized.
The looming mount
Had died again,
But now it stood
Immortalized.

SECURED BUT NOT SECURE

The fight went on
To March 16th,
When Iwo was
Declared "secured."
Sufficient ground
Was held to mark
The battle's outcome
As assured.

But both of the
Afflicted foes
Stayed victims of
Their bitter cup.
And thousands more
Were killed or maimed
In work that's known
As "mopping up."

Japanese prisoners. These men claimed to have been civilian workers on Iwo Jima who were conscripted when General Kuribayashi began his buildup.

Photo by Lou Lowery

Final casualties on the American side were 6,821 dead, 19,217 wounded, and 2,648 cases of combat fatigue.

At least 20,000 Japanese were either slaughtered— many by incineration—or killed themselves to avoid the dishonor of surrendering.

C- 2-28
5th Div., F. M. F.
C/o F. P. O., San Francisco
California, 2/4/45

Dear Dad ~

Am at sea, headed for a scrap. It's about time, don't you think?

In case I am not able to write for a while, don't worry. I'll be ok. Will write as soon as I can.

I'll be careful.

Bye

Dick

CPL. R. J. WHEELER

Author's note to his father as the battle loomed.

IN REPLYING ADDRESS
COMMANDANT OF THE MARINE CORPS
WASHINGTON 25. D. C.
AND REFER TO

SERIAL 359278
DGU-893-emk

HEADQUARTERS U. S. MARINE CORPS

WASHINGTON

31 March, 1945.

My dear Mr. Wheeler:

A report has just been received that your son, Corporal Richard J. Wheeler, USMCR, sustained lacerations of the head and leg in action against the enemy on 21 February, 1945 at Iwo Jima, Volcano Islands. The report further states that he was removed for medical treatment. His condition is reported to be good.

I fully realize your anxiety, and you may be sure that any word received will be sent to you at the earliest possible moment. In the meantime, you have all the information that has been reported to this Headquarters. May I ask that you help this office send out additional information promptly by writing only of changes of address.

Sincerely yours,

L. B. BROOKS,
Captain, U. S. Marine Corps.

Mr. Clarence E. Wheeler,
1388 Perkiomen Avenue,
Reading, Pennsylvania.

Letter received by author's father from Marine Corps Headquarters in Washington.

May - 30, 1945

Dear Wheeler;

I suppose you never even dreamed you would be receiving a letter from Howard's wife - and - under the circumstances - I'm sorry I'm the one to answer your letter to my husband.

Howard was Killed

on Iwo Jima - 9th of March - the official telegram is the only word we have - as yet - received. Although I'm hoping to receive a letter from some one of the boys who were with him those last days. As you know he was the sort who was so thoughtful about writing some buddies wife or Mother, even if they weren't killed or wounded - just if they showed up well in combat. So surely some one will now do the same for him. Although there's not very much consolation

in those sort of letters —
But I keep wondering
about it — anyway.
Howard wrote me
four lengthy letters from
Guam — One the day
before he was killed. In
this last letter he
told me you had been
wounded — and how very
sorry he was — as he said
to quote his letter "He is
probably one of the most
fundamentally honest
person there ever was.
I would trust him with
anything. He didn't
even want to go back
to the States, as he wants
to do his share of
combat until the war
is over. He would

never complain about anything – yet everyone liked him. I'm going to write to him to-day or to-morrow – I really do miss that guy. He was only with me three days on this Island But I expect to see him later." (End of quotation) Those were his exact words about you – and – he's mentioned you lots in previous letters.

At that time Harold Keller & Robeson were still with him – He said he had Been in the Command of a platoon for the last few days – & of course he was

Rather proud of that!!!
Hammer is at
Camp Pendleton now —
He had shrapnel wounds
in his side — Bob Lone
is in San Diego —
I sincerely hope you're
going to be perfectly O.K
before long — and Howard
would have appreciated
you remembering him by
writing. I've wondered
where you were & how.
You have plenty of time
for poetry now? Write
to me when you feel like
it — As Ever — Maxine Snyder

How the author learned of the death of Howard Snyder, his best friend.

Thursday evening
August 2nd 1945

Dear Wheeler —

Only this afternoon I received your battered and belated card of May 17th. Of course, I was delighted to hear from you, old man! Time and again I've wondered and inquired of you for as you know, that little group of (shall I say) intellectuals of the third plt. was pretty well shot up.

Say, how in blazes did you get yourself put in Carolina — that's not too far from Penna? Guess you know, Idaho is quite some walk from dear old Massachusetts.

How's the jaw and leg now? I don't have to tell you how damn sorry we all were that day you caught it. Snyder was plenty sore over it. When it came to digging in at night he was a bit lost without you, I saw that myself.

You know Wheeler, that day our pet. made the top of Suribachi and got the old flag up, I had a chat with Snyder and old Thomas the Tiger — poor Thomas, he was so dirty & tired, but magnificent after the way he led us when Wells was hit. He said it was one of his happiest moments, but that it would really be complete if ole Wheeler could have been with us & seen it all. Many times I heard he & Howard talk it over before they were killed — "Wheeler would have gloried in it, if he could have only been with us."

Yup, we really missed you & White.

I suppose you know I lost my boy, Rozek. I had him since the day he arrived from boot camp. Sure, he was big and one-way, but inside he was all man — he was a better man than I'll ever be, and Lord, but his Bar killed a lot of Japs before they finally got him!

As you, no doubt, know a sniper pluged me clean thru the middle as I was grenading a bunker up on the Northern end of the island. Keller was covering me and thanks to his clear headedness I'm alive, he saved my life by draging me to cover. He's in O.C.S. at Qontiqo (that's not the right spelling, is it?) The skipper put him up for it and he surely rates it.

From Iwo I went to an Army hospital at Siapan, then by air to Pearl, then to Frisco and up here to Farragut. I arrived here May 17th.

I've just returned from 37 days sick leave at home. Just at present I'm about 20 miles from the hospital back in the woods on lake Hayden at a delightful, rambling mansion, a sort of a rest camp.

I had pretty bad time of it for a few months, but luck was with me and I've come a long way from the 110 lbs. I sunk to. I'm in pretty fair shape. My hip is rather dead from the nerves that were knocked out where the slug came out my back, but we Yankees don't die easily, you know!

I'm all tanned & fattened up & ought to be back to duty in a month or so.

Hey, littlle "Chick" Robeson is in the next ward. He lost a finger & his Bar!

Well, this is enough for now; you must be bored, but do write and tell me all about yourself + the boys you have contacted.

I only hope this reaches you a little quicker than your card did me.

Thanks so far writing, old man, it is a fine thing to hear from, shall we say, a fellow artist and man-o-war?

Leader

Letter to author by Robert Leader about five months after the battle while the two friends were recuperating from severe wounds in hospitals about 2,500 miles apart. Immediately after the war the battered men—one an art student, the other an aspiring author—began working on their dream careers, which, living into their eighties, they managed to bring to fulfillment.

GENERAL HOLLAND M. SMITH
U. S. M. C. RETIRED
1821 VIKING WAY
LA JOLLA, CALIFORNIA

June 4, 1965

Mrs. Rosalie Brody
Publicity Manager
Thomas Y. Crowell Company
201 Park Avenue South
New York, N. Y.

My dear Mrs. Brody:

The delay in replying to your letter of 26 May was due to nine days in the Naval Hospital, San Diego, California. I was released on June 2nd.

I have read and reread the magnificent recreation of the part played by the 3rd Platoon, E Company, 2nd Battalion, 28th Marines as described by Mr. Richard Wheeler, who was a member of that historic platoon which fought so gallantly to raise the first American flag on the summit of Mount Suribachi.

At approximately noon on Friday, February 23, 1945, accompanied by the Secretary of the Navy, James Forrestal, on the beach below Suribachi, we witnessed the raising of the Second Flag on Suribachi. The Secretary turned to me and said "Holland, the raising of that flag means a Marine Corps for 500 years". Watching the raising of the flag which indicated the eventual capture of Iwo Jima was one of the proud moments of my life. No American could view this symbol of heroism and suffering without a lump in his throat. Nor will we ever forget those gallant Marines whose courage, loyalty, devotion to duty and fighting spirit resulted in the capture of Iwo Jima.

I recommend to every red-blooded man and woman in our nation that they read "The Bloody Battle for Suribachi" and be proud of his or her American heritage.

You are hereby authorized to use the contents of this letter for any purpose.

With best wishes for success,

1965 letter to the author's publisher by Iwo's top Marine commander, General Holland Smith, after he had been provided with an advance copy of *Suribachi*.

General Holland M. Smith—seated, wearing helmet—in a captured Japanese dugout.

Marine Corps Photo

Dear Mrs. Yoshii Kuribayashi:

This book is a gift to you from Charles Early, of Sarasota, Florida. I am delighted that he thought of this, and it is a pleasure for me to send it to you, and to include my respects and my compliments. Thank you very much for the good pictures you provided for the book. I am sure that you know by this time that the Americans considered your husband to be a great general. I myself am sorry that he had to die. Through my reading of the general's letters to you, I have come to feel that I almost know you, and it is very apparent to me that the great general had a great lady for a wife.

My best wishes to you and your family.

Sincerely yours,

Richard Wheeler

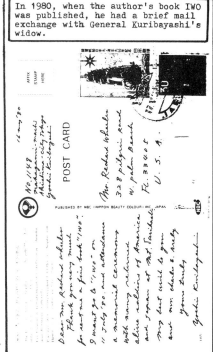

In 1980, when the author's book IWO was published, he had a brief mail exchange with General Kuribayashi's widow.

RECONCILIATION. (Begin reading in small box at upper right.)

MUSTER AT SUNSET

By November 2006, there were only nine members of Easy Company's 3rd Platoon still alive. Seven of us managed to make it to Washington, D.C., for a platoon reunion that was part of a four-day series of Veterans Day activities. Our seven-man reunion was sponsored by Texas Governor Rick Perry as a tribute to our Texas platoon leader, Keith Wells, now long-retired as an honorary major.

Wells was still hardy and strong-spirited at age 85. But he grew misty-eyed as he greeted the handful of old men, all wearing Purple Hearts, who had once rallied to his indomitable leadership and joined him in a costly but gainful charge into Suribachi's main defenses.

Among the highlights of the Veterans Day events was a White House breakfast, during which our 3rd Platoon men were photographed, individually, with President George W. Bush and First Lady Laura Bush.

Also on the Veterans Day schedule were two military banquets, the dedication of the Marine Corps museum at Quantico, services for the dead at Arlington, and gatherings at the new World War II Memorial in Washington.

Many thousands of veterans and civilians were in the Washington area for the round of activities, which were favored by perfect weather. Cameras clicked incessantly, and many were aimed at Keith Wells and his men, who were easily identified by special caps that proclaimed: "The 3rd Platoon—1st on Suribachi."

Most deeply rewarding to the seven Marines, however, was the camaraderie they enjoyed. Their terrifying days on Iwo Jima were discussed freely—sometimes even with touches of amusement. They considered themselves privileged to have been part of a vital mission that provided them an extraordinary adventure and national repute.

Slain comrades were mentioned lamentingly, but the general carnage was accepted as a natural part of warfare. The seven were proud of their wounds, and they shrugged off the residual problems and discomforts that have never stopped plaguing them.

They expressed satisfaction with the matter-of-fact way they had returned home and immediately began building productive lives, much too busy to be haunted very long by the ghosts of Iwo Jima.

To a man they agreed that, if they were young again and the nation called upon them to deal with another such challenge, they would respond at once.

The seven old men who were once proud Marines—and still are. From left: John Scheperle, James Rigney, Dick Wheeler, Chuck Lindberg, Keith Wells, Kenneth Espenes, and Bill Wayne.

Photo by Adam Makos, *Ghost Wings* magazine

Major Keith Wells, in company with the author's aide, his cousin Judge Jacqueline Russell, and the author.

Photo by Richard Sallee

The author (right) with his lifetime friend, Charles "Chuck" Lindberg, one of Iwo Jima's flag raisers, and the feat's only survivor. (Chuck died, nearly 87 years old, seven months after this meeting.)

Photo by Jacqueline L. Russell

Chuck Lindberg in 1944.

Studio Photo

John G. Scheperle as a teen-aged 3rd Platooner—always a MAN you could count on.

Studio Photo

William S. "Bill" Wayne as a college student in 1948.

Family Photo

Bob Lane, leader of the 2nd Squad, and his wife Scarlet, were unable to attend the 2006 reunion, but were sent caps that made them honorary members of the group.

Family Photo

At a Marine Corps birthday ball. General Peter Pace, Chairman of the Joint Chiefs of Staff (the first Marine in our nation's history to gain this position), is conversing with the author and Chuck Lindberg.

Photo by Jacqueline L. Russell

Taken at the White House on Veterans Day, 2006.

White House Photographer

INDEX